"If you are a human being in relationships, ⎡
to offer, with updated content; relatable, ⎣
audio-guided exercises and worksheets; and exercises you can try out on
your own, or with a partner. This edition includes essential skills for
healthy communication, negotiating with others, and improving interpersonal intimacy. Russ's writing style and insights bring compassion and
authenticity to life on every page."

> —**Sheri Turrell, PhD**, psychologist and psychoanalyst in
> Toronto, ON, Canada; adjunct faculty in the department
> of psychiatry at the University of Toronto; peer-reviewed
> acceptance and commitment therapy (ACT) trainer;
> and coauthor of *ACT for Adolescents*

"Having a successful relationship is hard work, especially given all the
myths about finding your one true soulmate. In this updated book, Russ
Harris explodes these myths and provides you with a practical handbook
to navigate the complexities of relationships in a realistic, heartfelt, and
meaningful way. You'll be given all the tools and techniques you need to
build your relationship and create a connection that is deep, fulfilling,
and lasting."

> —**Joe Oliver, PhD**, founder of Contextual Consulting,
> and coauthor of *The Mindfulness and Acceptance
> Workbook for Self-Esteem*

"A new, revised version of the ideal book for couples who want to
strengthen their relationship. In a step-by-step approach, this book offers
the reader a wealth of techniques to handle difficult thoughts and feelings; let go of unhelpful stories and tactics; and learn new skills for better
communicating, negotiating, and appreciating each other. A must-read
for anyone who wants to improve their relationship, and an invaluable
resource for professionals who work with couples."

> —**Maria Karekla, PhD**, licensed clinical psychologist,
> and associate professor in the department of psychology
> at the University of Cyprus

"Russ has done an incredible job teaching you how to nourish your relationship, even when things get rocky. You'll learn how to have deep, intimate moments with your partner; how to deal with conflict without destroying the relationship; how to handle those long-lasting differences; and how to love and be loved. This is a must-read for anyone that wants to have a caring, rich, and meaningful romantic relationship."

—**Patricia E. Zurita Ona, PsyD**, author of *Acceptance and Commitment Skills for Perfectionism and High-Achieving Behaviors* and *Living Beyond OCD Using Acceptance and Commitment Therapy*

"In this self-help book for individuals navigating relationship stress, Russ Harris does a masterful job of teaching ACT principles: to be in the moment, connect with your values, and improve your relationship. Broken into many brief topics, this book will help you in ways you didn't even know you needed. I highly recommended it for anyone in an intimate relationship."

—**Michael Twohig, PhD**, professor, and coauthor of *The Anxious Perfectionist*

"There seems to be an infinite number of books about building and maintaining solid, loving relationships with others. Few of them possess the evidence to justify their suggestions. Russ Harris offers something different—an evidence-based treatise that is simply profound. Change the way you view and approach relationships for the better. If more people read this book, the epidemic of loneliness would slowly dissipate."

—**Todd B. Kashdan**, author of *The Art of Insubordination*, and professor of psychology who leads The Well-Being Laboratory at George Mason University

"Relationship problems are some of the trickiest challenges that we all face! Understanding the nature of the human heart—as well as the science of human behavior—is critical if you are going to live with love and allow your life to flourish. Russ Harris provides you with the perfect blend of effective scientific methods and a deeply compassionate soul in ACT *with Love*. Life is hard, read Russ Harris."

> —**Dennis Tirch, PhD,** founding director of The Center
> for Compassion Focused Therapy, and associate clinical
> professor at Mt. Sinai Medical Center

"A warm and life-changing read, for people at any point in their relationship. Harris's writing style is witty and poignant, offering help on issues such as whether to continue with a relationship or end it, how to appreciate your partner, making repairs when things are off course, and developing intimacy. A must-read to enhance your connection with your loved one or to move on from a relationship that isn't working. I cannot recommend this book enough."

> —**Louise McHugh**, professor of psychology at University
> College Dublin, and coauthor of *The Self and Perspective Taking*

"The second edition of ACT *with Love* provides new guidance on core relationship skills—communication, negotiation, self-compassion, and more. I can imagine a world where I would be able to give this book to anyone ready to publicly commit to a loving relationship. I would offer it with this advice: 'Read it aloud with the person you love. Love is difficult and necessary and the very best in life. These are the secrets!'"

> —**Patti Robinson, PhD**, consultant, trainer, and coauthor
> of *The Depression Toolkit* and *The Mindfulness and Acceptance
> Workbook for Depression*

"We all wish to love and be loved, but this is hard to do. In this beautifully written and wise book, we learn how to cultivate deep, loving connection even when we face the inevitable challenges that any relationship brings. This book is a must-read for all couples who wish to create the conditions of deep and lasting love."

—**John P. Forsyth**, professor of psychology and director of the Anxiety Disorders Research Program at the University at Albany, SUNY; and coauthor of *The Mindfulness and Acceptance Workbook for Anxiety* and *Anxiety Happens*

"Beautifully written and easy to understand, the second edition of this highly successful book by a master developer of ACT is even more practical and relationship-enhancing. By diving into how ACT applies to a broader range of important interpersonal skills, this book gives you the tools you need to take your relationship to another level. Highly recommended."

—**Steven C. Hayes, PhD**, Nevada Foundation Professor of psychology at the University of Nevada, Reno; originator and codeveloper of ACT; and author of *A Liberated Mind*

"*ACT with Love* is jam-packed with practical and clear strategies for improving your relationship. Russ Harris is a world-renowned ACT trainer who teaches ACT in plain, simple, and easy-to-understand language, and this book truly does that—providing a much-needed resource. The many case studies are engaging, and the inclusion of self-compassion is wonderful. I highly recommend this book!"

—**Tamar D. Black, PhD**, educational and developmental psychologist, and author of *ACT for Treating Children*

ACT

with

Love

Fully Revised & Updated
SECOND EDITION

Stop Struggling, Reconcile Differences &
Strengthen Your Relationship with
Acceptance & Commitment Therapy

Russ Harris

New Harbinger Publications, Inc.

Publisher's Note

This publication is designed to provide accurate and authoritative information in regard to the subject matter covered. It is sold with the understanding that the publisher is not engaged in rendering psychological, financial, legal, or other professional services. If expert assistance or counseling is needed, the services of a competent professional should be sought.

NEW HARBINGER PUBLICATIONS is a registered trademark of New Harbinger Publications, Inc.

New Harbinger Publications is an employee-owned company.

Copyright © 2023 by Russ Harris
New Harbinger Publications, Inc.
5674 Shattuck Avenue
Oakland, CA 94609
www.newharbinger.com

All Rights Reserved

Cover design by Sara Christian; Acquired by Tesilya Hanauer; Edited by Karen Levy

---

Library of Congress Cataloging-in-Publication Data

Names: Harris, Russ, 1966- author.
Title: ACT with love : stop struggling, reconcile differences, and strengthen your relationship with acceptance and commitment therapy / by Russ Harris.
Description: 2nd edition. | Oakland, CA : New Harbinger Publications, Inc., [2023] | Includes bibliographical references.
Identifiers: LCCN 2023000806 | ISBN 9781648481635 (trade paperback)
Subjects: LCSH: Interpersonal relations. | Self-acceptance. | Love. | Acceptance and commitment therapy.
Classification: LCC HM1106 .H37 2023 | DDC 158.2--dc23/eng/20230310
LC record available at https://lccn.loc.gov/2023000806

Printed in the United States of America

25   24   23

10   9   8   7   6   5   4   3   2   1   First Printing

To Adrian and Margaret, for all your love, support, and encouragement and for enriching my life in so many, many ways, both tiny and vast.

Contents

Acknowledgments

Many heartfelt thanks all those friends, relatives, and colleagues who gave me invaluable feedback on the first edition of this book—Margaret Denman, Louise Hayes, Carmel Harris, Joe Parsons, Genghis Lloyd-Harris, Kim Paleg, and Joanne Steinwachs; and to my partner, Natasha, for all her help, support, love, and input for the second edition.

In addition, it's hard to express the enormous gratitude I feel toward Steve Hayes, the originator of ACT; gratitude which extends to Kelly Wilson, Kirk Strosahl, John Forsyth, Hank Robb, and the whole ACT community, as well as my agent, Sammie Justesen, and the entire team at New Harbinger—including Catharine Meyers, Michele Waters, Tracy Carlson, and Matt McKay. Plus, extra-special thanks to editors Jean Blomquist and Karen Levy for their great work in trimming the fat from the first and second editions of this book, respectively. And on top of all that, a super-duper-humongous vote of thanks to Tesilya Hanauer, the acquiring editor; without her enthusiasm and support, neither the first edition nor this new one would ever have happened.

Part 1

Getting Stuck

CHAPTER 1

Love Ain't Easy

Love and pain are intimate dance partners; they go hand in hand. Not always, of course. When your relationship is running smoothly, you're getting on well with each other, and those warm, fuzzy feelings are flowing freely—that's pretty wonderful. Such magical moments inspire zillions of poems, songs, books, shows, and movies. But the problem is: *those moments don't last.*

The fact is, in every relationship, sooner or later problems will arise. We'll have different wants and desires, competing needs and goals, opposing opinions and attitudes. At times we'll all screw up, make mistakes, or treat each other unkindly. Tension and conflict are inevitable, and when they occur, all those wonderful loving feelings fly out the window. And in their wake come anger, sadness, anxiety, guilt, disappointment, frustration, or other painful emotions.

Although at some level we all know this happens, we easily forget or dismiss it. We cling to those magical moments and blissful feelings and hope they will last forever. We buy into myths about "soul mates" and "perfect partners" and the idea that "love should be easy." We expect our partners to meet our needs, fulfill our wishes, make our lives easier—and then we get upset when reality clashes with fantasy.

And as if all that were not challenging enough, the people with whom we are closest are often the ones who "push our buttons" the most. While a snide remark, cold rejection, harsh criticism, or angry outburst may be unpleasant coming from our boss, a neighbor, or a coworker, it usually hurts far more when it comes from a loved one. In other words, love makes us vulnerable. When we allow ourselves to be close to and open with another—to let them past our defenses and into our heart—then we allow ourselves to get hurt.

The inconvenient truth is: relationships are both wonderful and dreadful. And while we all appreciate the upside of a close, loving relationship, most of us struggle to deal effectively with the downside. In fact, often when a relationship becomes painful, the things we do to try to fix things just make it worse. So it's hardly surprising that divorce rates are sky-high, people increasingly fear long-term commitment, and there are more single adults than ever before. And as for those relationships that *do* last, many are less than satisfactory: full of emptiness, loneliness, and misery.

Does this all sound a bit grim, gloomy, and depressing? Fear not. The good news is, there's a powerful, practical, science-based way to bring some order to this messy business. It's called…

Acceptance And Commitment Therapy

This book is based on a powerful model of psychology known as acceptance and commitment therapy, or ACT. Pronounced as the word "act" (not as the initials A.C.T.), the ACT model was created in the United States by psychologist Steven Hayes and his colleagues, Kirk Strosahl and Kelly Wilson (Hayes, Strosahl, and Wilson 1999). The basic aims of ACT are to reduce psychological suffering and build a rich and meaningful life—and there's a wealth of scientific evidence to show it works.

More than three thousand published studies show ACT's effectiveness with a vast range of painful human conditions, from depression and anxiety to addiction and trauma; and we can readily apply the core ACT principles to just about any relationship issue. As a bonus, although this book focuses on couples, you can use the same strategies to repair, strengthen, and enrich any important close relationship, whether that's with your children, parents, friends, or relatives.

There are three parts to the book. In part 1, Getting Stuck, we look at common challenges in relationships, and the frequent dilemma of whether to leave or stay. In part 2, Getting Real, you'll identify the main problems in your relationship, including an honest look at how you may have contributed to them. And in part 3, Getting Active, we'll go through the practicalities of how to build a close and loving relationship—and deal effectively with all the difficult thoughts and feelings that inevitably arise during that process.

Will this approach work for everyone? Well, in my twenty-plus years as a therapist, I've worked with literally thousands of people who found it very helpful. But it doesn't work for *everyone*. Sometimes the damage that's been done is irreparable, or the partners have grown so far apart that there's no coming back, or the relationship itself is so toxic that ending it is the only sensible option. This is why there's an appendix at the back of the book titled: "If All Else Fails: How to Leave Your Relationship." However, I'm pleased to report that while there are no guarantees, most people do get good results. (Note: This book is geared toward commonplace relationship issues, of the sort that virtually everyone has at times. It's not for severe issues such as domestic violence.)

Myths About Love

Of course, applying ACT to our relationships isn't easy. It's often quite a challenge. And that challenge is all the greater because of all the stuff and nonsense that's been pumped into our heads over the years. From our very first fairy tales, in which the prince and princess lived happily ever after, to the Hollywood endings of most popular movies, books, and TV shows, we hear and see the same old myths again and again. Here are the big three:

Myth 1: The Perfect Partner

Did you know that somewhere out there, in the big wide world, there is a perfect match for you? The partner of your dreams, who will fulfill all your fantasies, meet all your needs, and live with you in everlasting bliss.

Yeah, right. And Santa Claus is real too.

Truth is, there's no such thing as the perfect partner, just as there's no such thing as the perfect couple. (As the old joke goes, there are only two types of couples: those who have a wonderful relationship, and those whom you know really well.) But how hard is it to truly let go of this idea? Have you ever found yourself comparing your partner to others? Dwelling on their faults and flaws and shortcomings? Thinking about how life would be so much better if only they would change? Fantasizing about the partner you could or should have had? At times we all get caught up in these ways of thinking, and it's a recipe for frustration, anger, disappointment, and numerous other forms of misery.

Myth 2: Love Should Be Easy

So, love should be easy, should it? Hmmmmm. Let's look at this proposition more closely.

When you live intimately for a long period of time with another human being who has (a) different thoughts and feelings, (b) different interests, (c) different expectations about housework, sex, money, religion, parenting, holidays, work-life balance, and quality time, (d) different styles for communicating, negotiating, and self-expression, (e) different reactions to the things that you enjoy or fear or detest, (f) different drives for food, sex, sport, play, and work, (g) different standards of cleanliness and tidiness, (h) friends and relatives that you don't get on with too well, and (i) lifelong, deeply entrenched habits and quirks that annoy you...it should be easy?

Does that sound convincing to you?

Of course, our minds are quick to point out that if our partners were more compatible, if they didn't have so many differences from us, then our relationships would be much easier. Good point, but now we're right back to myth 1: the perfect partner. The fact is there will always be significant differences between you and your partner in some or all of the areas mentioned here and also in many others. That's why relationships *aren't* easy. They require communication, negotiation, compromise, and a lot of acceptance of differences; they also require you to stand up for yourself, to be honest about your desires and your feelings, and—in some situations, where something vitally important to your health and well-being is at stake—to absolutely refuse to compromise. This is quite a challenge. But as long as you expect your partner to think and feel and act just like you, you're setting yourself up for disappointment and frustration.

Now there's no denying, some couples have more in common than others. Some couples are naturally optimistic, calm, and easygoing. Some couples have excellent communication skills. Some couples have very similar interests. And let's face it, if you're both passionately mad about rock climbing, it's a lot easier to agree on your vacation plans than if one of you loves sunbathing on the beach and the other absolutely hates it. But no matter how much you have in common, there will always be differences that challenge you. (Later in the book, you'll learn how to stop struggling and make peace with these differences, thereby dissolving much frustration and resentment.)

Myth 3: Everlasting Love

Usually when people talk about "love," they mean an emotional state: a wonderful mix of thoughts, feelings, and sensations. The problem with defining love this way is that feelings don't last very long. Just as the clouds above continually change—shrinking, growing, dispersing, and reappearing—so do our emotions. Thus, as long as we define love as a feeling, it can never be everlasting.

Of course, in the early days of a relationship, those feelings of love are more intense, last longer, and come back more quickly than they do later on. We commonly call this "the honeymoon phase" of a relationship, when we are totally intoxicated by those Romeo-and-Juliet, head-over-heels-in-love feelings. This phase doesn't last long—only six to eighteen months for most relationships, and rarely more than three years. And when it is over, we generally experience a sense of loss. After all, it *does* feel good! So good, in fact, that when the honeymoon phase ends, many people break up with their partners, reasoning, "I don't feel in love anymore, so clearly this is not the right partner for me. I'm out of here."

This is a great pity, because often an authentic, loving, deeply committed relationship only develops once the honeymoon phase is over. In the honeymoon phase, it's as if you're on a drug that intoxicates you and plays with your senses. And when you're "high," your partner seems wonderful. But you're not seeing reality; you're seeing a drug-induced fantasy. And when the drug wears off, you see your partner as they really are. You suddenly realize that the knight's shining armor is covered in rust spots, and his white horse is really a gray donkey. Or the maiden's pure silk dress is actually cheap nylon, and her long golden locks are really a wig. Naturally this comes as a bit of a shock. But herein lies the opportunity to build an authentic intimate relationship between two people who see each other as they really are. And as this relationship develops, there will be new feelings of love—perhaps not as intense or intoxicating, but potentially much richer and more fulfilling.

Moving Beyond the Myths

There are many other common love myths. (For example, "My partner should always know what I want or how I feel; I shouldn't have to tell them.") And if we use these myths as a guide for our relationships, we set ourselves up for a painful struggle with reality. A struggle that reality always wins.

So what's the alternative? A miserable relationship where we "settle for what we've got," "suck it up," and "get on with it"? Far from it. My aim in this book is to help you create the best relationship you possibly can—one in which you treat each other with love, kindness, and consideration, make peace with your differences, appreciate what you each have to offer, handle your emotions more effectively, support each other to thrive and learn and grow, and make the most of the time you spend together.

Does that sound unbelievable? If so, good! Throughout this book, I encourage you not to believe anything just because I say so. Instead, test these ideas out and see what happens. Treat every exercise, every skill, every strategy as an experiment. They are in the book because I expect them to be helpful—but we need to be realistic; nothing works every single time; nothing works for everyone; nothing is 100 percent guaranteed. So play around with the tools, techniques, and strategies within these pages; test them out and carefully observe what happens. If you try something and it has the desired results, stick with it. If not, drop it, and try something else. And very importantly, if you're ever feeling stuck or frustrated, remind yourself of...

What's in Your Control

Our aim in ACT is to help you make the most of your life—and the more you learn to focus on what is in your control, the more empowerment and fulfillment you will experience. In contrast, the more you focus on what's *out* of your control, the more disempowered, dissatisfied, or disappointed you'll be. So when it comes to your relationship, it's important to know what's in your control and what isn't.

For example, can you control your partner? Ha! You wish! In part 3 of the book, you'll learn skills for *influencing* your partner's behavior—but you'll never be able to *control* them. And when you apply these influencing skills in your relationship, here's what will happen: either your partner's behavior will change—or it won't. There's a good chance it will, but no guarantee.

Note: Whenever I use the words "influence" and "influencing," they have a specific meaning: "influencing in considerate, honest, *caring* ways that are healthy for your relationship, and good for the well-being of both parties." If one partner uses methods such as aggression, lying, deceiving, gaslighting, threatening, intimidating, the "silent treatment," or other methods that are disrespectful, dishonest, or detrimental to the well-being of the other—I will call this "manipulation," rather than "influence." It's a very important distinction; manipulating your partner may get your needs met, but it's not healthy for your partner or your relationship. In contrast, knowing how to constructively influence your partner's behavior, in honest, fair, and considerate ways, is fundamental to building a healthy relationship.

Okay, so you can't *control* your partner, but you can *influence* them. How? Through what you say and what you do. So if you want to successfully influence your partner's behavior, you need to first take control of *your own* behavior: control over what you say and what you do. The more you can control your own words and actions, the better your ability to constructively influence your partner.

And therein lies a problem. When we're feeling reasonably good, and the situation isn't that challenging, it's relatively easy to take control of our actions. But the more challenging the situation, and the more difficult the thoughts and feelings showing up, the more likely we are to lose control over what we say and do, and act in ways that further strain the relationship—such as yelling, blaming, criticizing, name-calling, or "giving the cold shoulder" or "the silent treatment."

Now it's a given that difficult thoughts and feelings will show up when there are problems in your relationship; you can't expect to feel happy, content, and relaxed amid ongoing tension and conflict. But you can learn new skills to take the power and impact out of all of those painful thoughts and feelings; to "unhook" yourself from them, so they can't bring you down, overwhelm you, or jerk you around. Much of this book involves learning such skills—and the stronger they become, the more control you'll have over your actions. And greater control over your actions will enable you to not only influence your partner more successfully, but also to behave more like the sort of partner you want to be. It will help you cut back on things you say and do that stress your relationship, and enable you to do things that improve it instead.

The Journey Ahead

There are three main objectives for the journey ahead:

1. To get clear on the sort of partner you really want to be, and use that knowledge to do things that strengthen your relationship (while cutting back on doing things that drain it).

2. To learn new skills for handling difficult thoughts and feelings more effectively, taking the impact and power out of them so they can't jerk you around.

3. To learn new skills for constructively influencing your partner's behavior, in ways that are healthy for you, your partner, and your relationship.

As you work through the book, we'll tackle these aims in the order listed previously. I know many readers would prefer to start at 3, influencing your partner, but that's not a good idea. Why not? Because until you've got 1 and 2 in place (i.e., you can handle your thoughts and feelings and behave like the partner you want to be), it's almost impossible to do 3 successfully. So I urge you to please be patient, and go with the flow. Let's start off with an important question...

CHAPTER 2

Should I Stay or Should I Go?

I can't stand it anymore. I have to get out of this relationship.

Have you ever had a thought like that? Me too. Truth is, almost everybody has thoughts like this at times. You see, the human mind is, at its core, a problem-solving machine. The moment it encounters a problem, it immediately looks for a solution. And when a situation is painful, difficult, or threatening, then one perfectly reasonable solution is: *get out of there!* And for sure, there are *some* problematic situations where "getting out of there" is clearly the best solution—for example, when your building is on fire! But in relationships, it's rarely as clear as that, so many people struggle with the big dilemma: *Should I stay or should I go?*

Shortly, we'll look at how to resolve that dilemma; first let's recap some essential knowledge about relationships that you learned very early in life.

What You Learned In Kindergarten

You may be surprised to find that you learned the fundamentals for building good relationships while you were still at kindergarten. For example:

- Mind your manners
- Say please
- Say thank you
- Say sorry
- Listen carefully

- Tell the truth
- Don't interrupt
- Don't shout
- Don't push
- Don't hit

- Don't lie
- Don't call names
- Play fairly
- Be kind

- Take turns
- Wait patiently
- Share
- Pick up after yourself

Beneath the surface of these simple rules for kids, you'll find essential principles for building healthy relationships. In particular, these rules all point to the fundamental importance of treating each other fairly and considerately. In other words, they encourage us to respect each other's rights. If we want any relationship to thrive—whether it's with your partner, friends, family, coworkers, and so on—it's essential to know not only what *our* rights are, but also those of the other person involved. Knowing our rights enables us to gauge whether we are being treated fairly and considerately, *and* whether we're doing the same for the other party. So let's take a quick look at...

Your Bill of Rights

I invite you to read through this list of your fundamental rights in relationships. (Note: there is no one universally agreed set of relationship rights; if you Google it, you'll find many different lists of varying lengths. However, the ones I've selected crop up repeatedly.) Please carefully consider each right—and notice your own reactions. Do you agree, or disagree? Do uncomfortable feelings show up? Are there any rights you've forgotten or neglected, or others you've never considered?

- I have the right to be treated fairly and considerately.
- I have the right to make my needs equally important to those of others.
- I have the right to decline requests, provided I do so in a way that is fair and considerate.
- I have the right to be fallible, imperfect, and make mistakes.
- I have the right to ask for what I want, provided I do so in a way that is fair and considerate.

- I have the right to feel the way I feel.

- I have the right to honestly state my thoughts, feelings, ideas, and opinions in a way that is fair and considerate.

- I have the right to stand up for my rights, provided I do so fairly, with consideration of the rights of others.

Of course, your partner has all the same rights as you do—and respecting each other's rights is essential for a healthy relationship. If your rights are consistently ignored or dismissed, that won't be healthy for you or the relationship, and it's likely to raise the dilemma:

Should I Stay or Should I Go?

It's not uncommon for people to spend huge chunks of their day, completely lost in their thoughts, endlessly debating all the pros and cons of staying in or leaving their relationship. The problem is, there's no vitality in this. While you are bogged down in your own thought processes, fruitlessly replaying the big debate—*should I stay or should I go?*—you are wasting huge amounts of time and energy and missing out on your life.

Naturally if your relationship is unhealthy, and your basic rights are being ignored, it's important to consider the pros and cons of leaving. But dwelling on this dilemma repeatedly throughout the day, going over and over it in your head, is only likely to stress you out without helping you reach a clear decision. So you may find it helpful to consider that there are basically three options for responding to any problematic relationship:

Option 1: Leave.

Option 2: Stay and live by your values: do what you can to improve things, make room for the pain that goes with it, and treat yourself kindly.

Option 3: Stay—but do things that either make no difference or make it worse.

Let's take a look at each option.

Option 1: Leave

Would your overall quality of life be better if you left than if you stayed? Based on your current life circumstances—your income, location, marital status, children (or lack of them), family and social networks, age, health, religious beliefs, and so on—is it likely that your health and well-being would be better, in the long run, if you left? Of course, you can never know this for certain, but you can make a reasonable prediction based on what has happened up to this point.

I hope you will try everything in this book—really put your heart and soul into making your relationship work—before seriously considering this option. (Obviously there are exceptions—for example, if you are in physical danger from your partner—but as mentioned previously, such serious issues are beyond the scope of this book.) If you do give it your best shot and you still ultimately choose to leave, then you at least have the consolation of knowing you tried your hardest to make it work. (The appendix of this book describes how to leave your relationship in a way that minimizes damage. I hope you never have to read it.)

Option 2: Stay and Live by Your Values

If you can't or won't leave, or don't see it as a viable option right now, your best chance of improving your relationship lies in option 2: do what you can to make things better. As discussed earlier, in any relationship, what you have most control over are your own words and actions. So take control of your own words and actions and use them to constructively influence your partner and build a better relationship. Actively work at making things as good as they possibly can be, using the many strategies we'll explore later.

And of course, you can't expect to feel happy when there's tension and conflict in your relationship. The bigger the problem(s), the more painful the thoughts and feelings you'll have. So the other part of option 2—make room for your pain, and treat yourself kindly—is essential. Soon you'll learn how to "make room" for difficult thoughts and feelings—to take away their power and let them "flow through you"—while supporting yourself in a kind and caring way.

Option 3: Stay—But Either Do Things That Make No Difference or Make It Worse

All too often people stay in a problematic relationship, but instead of actively working to improve it, they worry, stew, ponder, blame, judge, analyze it to death, complain to others, or obsess about it. Or they become cold and withdrawn, or hostile and aggressive, or critical and judgmental. Or they passively comply with whatever their partner wants, and completely give up on their own needs and desires. Or they lie, deceive, and manipulate to get what they want. Or they try to avoid their painful feelings by taking drugs, drinking alcohol, smoking cigarettes, eating junk food, zoning out in front of the TV, surfing the internet, gambling, having affairs, shopping, and so on.

Yup, there's no shortage of things we can do that either don't help or make things worse. And even though we know it sucks the life out of our relationship, at times we all do it!

There's No Way Not to Choose

When you're facing the "stay or go" dilemma, there is no way *not to* choose. Until the day you actually leave this relationship, you're choosing to stay in it. So for each day you remain, ask yourself: What will I choose for today: option 2 or option 3? The more you choose option 2, the better your chances of improving things. And the more you choose option 3, the worse things will get. (And if you say, "I can't choose," that's the same as choosing option 3.)

"That's all very well," I hear you say, "but what happens if I choose option 2, and I do all the work, while my partner makes no effort at all?" Well, the good news is, your relationship is likely to improve even if you're the only one working at it.

However, there's no doubt the best results happen when both partners actively work at it. So watch out for statements like this: "I can't change my behavior. That's just what I do. I've always done that. You can't teach an old dog new tricks. You need to accept it." There is no scientific basis for such claims. We actually *can* teach old dogs new tricks. And humans are much smarter than dogs. Using the scientifically validated methods of ACT, we can all change our behavior, if we want to.

In a similar vein, it doesn't bode well if your partner's attitude is something like this: "I'm fine. I don't need to change. You're the one with the issues. I'm happy with the way I am. Sort yourself out and we'll be fine." If that's your partner's attitude, it's a red flag. If they can't or won't acknowledge how they contribute to the problems, are unable to see things from your perspective, are dismissive of your thoughts and feelings, and refuse to look at or work on their own behavior, those are truly massive obstacles to building the sort of relationship you really want.

So if that's what ultimately happens, after trying everything in this book, then you face a difficult choice: Stay or leave? However, if you do choose to leave at that point, at least you'll know you gave it your best shot. And furthermore, you'll have developed some useful new skills that will help you in other relationships—with your friends, family, and any future partner. On the other hand, if neither of you do any work—if you both choose option 3—then your relationship's sure to go from bad to worse.

Given you're reading this book, I'm assuming you have chosen option 2 (at least for today), so let's move on to part 2, and get real about the issues in your relationship.

Part II

Getting Real

CHAPTER 3

What's Your Problem?

Indira: We used to have fun together—going away for weekends, having people over for dinner, partying. Now all he's interested in is watching sports on TV. I want some fun!

David: He seems to think I'm made out of money. Spend, spend, spend. He buys these useless bits and pieces—clothes, books, kitchen stuff. Even a new TV. He doesn't seem to realize we have a mortgage to pay off.

Jane: He's not interested in sex anymore. He comes to bed after I'm asleep, gets up before I'm awake. I know I've put on some weight since I had the kids, but…

Demetri: She won't listen to reason. It's always got to be on her terms. She's right. She knows. My way or the highway. And if she doesn't get what she wants, believe you me—heads will roll!

Maria: She's so angry all the time. As soon as she gets in after work, she's snappy, grumpy, complaining about everything, flying off the handle when things aren't exactly how she wants them. There's no pleasing her.

Jason: She's turned into the ice maiden. She won't even let me touch her. As soon as I get near her, she's like, "Get away from me!"

Denise: He's never home. He's always at the office, or out with his friends, or working on his car. And when he is there, he never listens. He's always off in his own head.

Do any of these complaints sound vaguely familiar? Over many years, working with people from a wide variety of backgrounds, I've heard my clients criticize their partners for just about anything you can imagine— from having bad breath to having bad taste; from having no friends to having too many; from talking too much, to talking too little; from "obsessively cleaning" to "never doing any housework at all." Let's face it: the number of ways in which we can find fault with our partners is almost infinite. So what's the problem in your relationship?

Are you fighting, sulking, avoiding each other? Are you having disagreements about sex, money, housework, having kids, parenting styles, moving house? Are you feeling lonely, unloved, rejected, put down, nagged, or bullied? Are you bored? Are you under pressure from family, health, work, or financial issues? Are you struggling to cope with a major life challenge involving children, illness, job loss, legal action, retirement, or something else? Are you stressed out and "taking it out" on each other?

By the end of this book, you'll have the necessary tools to effectively deal with all these problems and more. And a good first step is to recognize that...

Differences Are Normal

Most of us have had thoughts at times like, "If only my partner were more like me, things would be so much easier." And there may be some truth in that. But that's not reality. The fact is, there are many, many differences between you and your partner. And that's hardly surprising, because you've been raised by different families, from whom you learned many different lessons about relationships. To better understand this, let's take a quick look at...

Attachment Theory

John Bowlby, an influential British psychiatrist, is best known as the originator of "attachment theory" (Bowlby 1969). To understand this theory, which helps us makes sense of many relationship issues, consider a newborn infant. Infants are born with strong instincts to seek out and stay close to caregivers who will protect and nurture them. This is essential for survival. An infant is entirely dependent on its caregivers, and without their ongoing protection and nurture, it will quickly die. (I use the term "caregiver" because not everyone is raised by their parents.) So, to use Bowlby's terminology, infants make "bids" to their caregivers for closeness, companionship, comfort, protection, caretaking, reassurance, and sustenance. At birth, the basic bids are crying, whimpering, or screaming—but as a child grows, they develop many other strategies to get protection, comfort, and nurture.

If a caregiver responds well to these bids—consistently and reliably providing nurture, comfort, protection, and sustenance—the child feels secure in that relationship. And this relationship then acts as a model for others. Basically, the child gets the idea that close relationships are safe, and the other person is likely to be caring, trustworthy, and dependable. This creates a kind of blueprint for positive, healthy, intimate relationships in later life: a "secure attachment style." As an adult, the attitude toward one's partner tends to be something like this: "I love you, I care about you, and I'm okay with that. I can handle a bit of tension or conflict between us because I know that's part and parcel of a loving relationship."

But what happens when a caregiver is not reliable and responsive, but repeatedly ignores the child's bids, or responds with hostility? Obviously, no caregiver is perfect, but if their tendency is to act in this way often and repeatedly, the child will *not* feel secure in that relationship. They will feel *insecure* and get the idea that close relationships are unsafe. Let's consider some examples of "insecure attachment."

Suppose a caregiver is very inconsistent. They often respond positively to the child's bids, but equally often, they ignore them. The child becomes insecure and anxious in that relationship—very uncertain about whether their needs will be met or not. In later life, this often leads to yearning for attention in relationships and "clinginess," possessiveness, or jealousy. As an adult, the attitude toward one's partner is something like this: "I'm worried you might not love me, or you might leave me, and I don't know if I can rely on you. I'm scared you're going to reject or abandon me. I really need to know for sure that you love me, and you won't leave me."

Now consider what happens if the caregiver only rarely responds positively to the child's bids; most of the time they are distant and disengaged and ignore the child's needs. In response, the child becomes emotionally distant, comes to expect that their needs won't be met, and often gives up trying. As adults, they tend to avoid seeking nurture, closeness, or caring in relationships and are therefore often lonely. In fact, often they prefer to avoid relationships altogether. As an adult, the attitude toward one's partner often goes something like this: "I'm scared you're going to neglect me, ignore my needs, let me down, or take me for granted. I'm scared to care about you deeply or get too close to you—because if I do, I'll end up disappointed, hurt, or lonely."

Finally, consider the case where a caregiver occasionally responds positively, but most of the time, they respond with aggression or hostility. As a result, the child is confused and doesn't know how to get their needs met. When around their caregivers, these children appear wary, anxious, or dazed. As adults, they find it hard to trust; they are fearful of being hurt, and closeness brings high levels of anxiety. They often have difficulty forming relationships, and the ones they have are usually brief. As an adult, the attitude toward one's partner is likely to be something like this: "I don't really know what to expect from this relationship. But I do know that getting close to you scares me. I'm scared you might hurt or harm me."

Now before we go any further, two very important points. First, you can have different attachment styles with different caregivers. Suppose your mother was mostly loving, supportive, and kind, but your father had little time or love for you; you'd probably be secure in your attachment to your mother, but insecure with your father. Second, your attachment style can change over the years, through therapy, coaching, personal growth, or what you learn and experience in later relationships.

Now there's a whole lot more to attachment theory; we've barely scratched the surface. So if it intrigues you, Google it. But please do be careful; it's easy to spend a lot of time combing through your childhood experiences, trying to figure out how they "made you the way you are." And while it's useful to have some understanding of how your childhood has influenced you, be wary of getting lost in "analysis paralysis": so busy analyzing your past experiences and figuring out "how you got to be this way" that you don't do anything practical about changing your behavior.

The main thing I hope you'll take from the outline is this: our earliest relationships profoundly influence the way we think, feel, and behave in future relationships. And because your early relationships were different than your partner's, you both came into this relationship with very different "blueprints," which give rise to differing ideas and expectations. But that's not the only explanation for your differences; we also need to consider…

What You Learned Growing Up

As you grew up you were exposed to a vast range of ideas about relationships: what to expect from them, what makes them work, what harms them, how to get your needs met, what your role is, what your partner's role is, and so on.

You picked up many ideas from your friends, your family, your school, your workplace, your hobbies, the various groups you belonged to, the books you read, the movies you watched, the music you listened to, the conversations you had, and the way you saw people treat each other in the world around you.

In addition, many of your ideas were shaped by your culture, your religion, your society, your social class, your political affiliation, your nationality, the gender you identify with, and so on.

You also learned a lot through experiment. You see, the truth is we're all control freaks at heart; we all like to get what we want. It's easy to see this in little children as they go through the "terrible twos." Toddlers want to get their own way, and when they don't, they may cry, yell, stamp their feet, throw themselves on the floor, sulk, hold their breath, throw their toys across the room, bite, hit, pull your hair, or shout, "I hate you, Mommy!" They'll do anything they can think of to try to get their own way.

We all experiment with such methods early in life, and if we find something that works, we keep doing it. Then, as we grow older, we develop and elaborate on these methods, and when the going get tough, we tend to fall back on them: calling names, snapping, yelling, threatening, storming off, the "silent treatment," and so on. That's why when an adult is "at their worst," we often describe them as "acting like a child." And because you and your partner both did many different experiments in your previous relationships, and both got different results from doing so, you naturally came to different conclusions about what you can expect from your partner and what the best ways are to get your needs met.

However, even that's not enough to explain all your differences. There's also your biological makeup to consider: your physical bodies, and the nervous systems within them, react *differently* to each other. You will both find different things pleasurable, or frightening, or interesting, or boring. Of course, you'll also share many similarities in your reactions, but the differences are inevitable. It's normal for you both to enjoy different foods, music, books, and movies; different types of touch; different types of sexual activity; and so on. It's natural and expected to have different desires, urges, passions, fears, and interests.

Inevitably, then, at this point in your life, you have many ideas, beliefs, desires, expectations, opinions, and feelings that are different from those of your partner. And that doesn't make yours "right" and theirs "wrong"—or vice versa; it just means *they're different*. Differences are normal, natural, and inevitable, and they don't need to be a problem, *if* we respond to them flexibly. Note the "*if*" in that sentence. All too often, we *don't* respond flexibly to the differences that show up in our relationships. Let's look at what we do instead.

The DRAIN on Your Relationship

When problems arise in our relationships, we often respond "inflexibly": in ineffective ways that make our problems worse or create new ones! There are five patterns of inflexible responding involved, at least to some extent, in almost every relationship issue. We can remember them with the acronym DRAIN:

D—Disconnection

R—Reactivity

A—Avoidance

I—Inside-the-mind

N—Neglecting values

Let's quickly go through these.

Disconnection

Have you ever felt a special connection with someone? Presumably you did with your partner (at least in the early days). The word "connection" comes from the Latin terms *com*, meaning "together," and *nectere*, meaning "to bind." Thus when we connect with someone, it's as if something binds us together, unites us in some special way. When we connect with someone, we are psychologically present; in other words, we are right here with them, in this moment, fully engaged.

To connect deeply with another human being, we need to give them our full attention, with an attitude of openness, warmth, and genuine curiosity. When someone pays attention to us in this way, we feel important, welcomed, appreciated. But when someone *disconnects* from us; when they're withdrawn, cold, or closed off; when they're so caught up in their own thoughts and feelings that they have no interest in us; when they seem bored, resentful, or distracted in our presence; when they treat us like a nuisance, intrusion, or irritant—well, that doesn't feel so good, does it?

If you disconnect frequently from your partner—or vice versa—the warmth, closeness, and intimacy drains from your relationship, leaving a vast, cold, empty space between you.

Reactivity

Bob is playing "monkeys" with his three-year-old son, Daniel. Daniel shrieks with delight as Bob swings him around while making chimp noises. It's all fun and games...until that horrifying moment when Bob drops him.

Daniel hits the floor with a thud. A moment of stunned silence, then he screws up his face and howls like a banshee. His mother, Sarah, rushes over, flustered and red-faced. "You're so irresponsible!" she snaps at Bob. She scoops Daniel up in her arms. "It's okay. You're okay. What did Daddy do to you?" As she pats Daniel's back, she glares at Bob.

Bob is furious. As far as he's concerned, Sarah's reaction is totally unfair. "You are such a bitch!" he yells, as he storms out the door.

Both Bob and Sarah are being "reactive." In reactive mode, we get hooked by our thoughts and feelings, and jerked around like a fish on the end of a line. We lack self-awareness, and have little or no conscious control of our actions. We act impulsively, mindlessly, or automatically: driven blindly by our emotions, blinkered by our own beliefs and judgments. Reactivity is especially common when emotions like anger, frustration, or resentment arise within us. These strong emotions instantly hook us, and we react by snapping, shouting, yelling, insulting, judging, criticizing, blaming, or making threats. The more reactive a partner is, the more likely they are to act in ways that strain and suffocate the relationship.

Avoidance

Human beings do not like unpleasant feelings. We all try hard to avoid them. This is completely natural, but it can create problems. A wealth of scientific research shows that the more effort we expend on avoiding unpleasant feelings, the worse our life tends to get. "Experiential avoidance" is the technical term for trying to avoid or get rid of unwanted "inner experiences," such as thoughts, feelings, memories, urges, and so on. Research shows us that higher levels of experiential avoidance directly correlate with greater risks of depression, anxiety, stress, addiction, and many other health issues.

Why should this be? Well, it's largely due to the strategies we use for avoiding those unwanted inner experiences—strategies like putting stuff into our bodies, distracting ourselves, or retreating to the comfort zone. Let's take a quick look at these now.

Putting stuff into our bodies. Humans are experts at this—filling their bodies with substances to make themselves feel good: chocolate, pizza, beer, wine, cigarettes, marijuana, heroin, Xanax, Ecstasy, French fries, and ice cream, to name but a few. These substances give us short-term relief from unpleasant feelings. But in the long run, if we overuse them, they wreak havoc on our health and well-being.

Distracting ourselves. When we're feeling bad, we often try to "take our mind off it." We distract ourselves with anything and everything: from TV, computers, and social media, to partying hard, burying ourselves in work, or going for a walk. Distraction helps us avoid unpleasant feelings in the short term, but it's often detrimental to our quality of life. Why? First, because of wasted time. How much time have you wasted in your life watching TV, surfing the net, scrolling through social media, or reading trashy magazines as a way to avoid boredom, anxiety, or loneliness? Imagine if you had invested that time pursuing things that were truly important and meaningful to you. Second, while we're busy distracting ourselves, we're not taking effective action to improve our quality of life. This is incredibly common in relationships. Rather than learning new skills to improve the way we interact with our partner, we busy ourselves with distraction.

Staying in the comfort zone. Challenging situations give rise to unpleasant feelings, such as fear, anxiety, anger, sadness, or frustration. One way to avoid these feelings is to avoid the situations that trigger them. So, for example, you may refuse to talk to your partner. Or refuse to listen to them. Or refuse to share a bed. Or leave the room. Or end the conversation. Or put off having that difficult conversation. Now obviously there's a time and a place for avoiding challenging situations. For example, if a conflict starts to escalate, it can be a good idea to call "time-out" and allow both of you to cool down before continuing. But if you habitually run away from dealing with the challenging issues in your relationship, it will suffer in the long run.

Sometimes this takes the form of "passivity" and "people pleasing": you give in to your partner, put their needs first, give up on your own desires and wishes, and do what you can to please them, to avoid any tension or conflict. And of course, for a relationship to thrive, there are times we'll need to compromise and put our partner's needs before our own; but if you're doing this excessively and repeatedly, you'll be stressed out, burned-out, or miserable. (It's a common contributing factor to depression and anxiety.)

In everyday language, we call this "staying in the comfort zone." But that's not a great term, because living in this way isn't comfortable. When we spend too much time in the comfort zone, we feel stuck, weighed down, despondent. We should call it "the stagnant zone" or the "missing-out-on-life zone." For our relationships to grow and thrive, we need to face up to many challenging situations, and make room for the difficult thoughts and feelings they bring. If we frequently avoid these situations, our relationship will inevitably stagnate.

Of course, we're all avoidant to some degree, and a little bit of avoidance isn't a problem. But the greater the degree to which one or both partners avoid, the more issues it creates.

Inside-the-Mind

Minds like to chatter. They have a lot to say that's useful and important—but a heck of a lot more that is unhelpful and unimportant. If you were to write down every single thought that goes through your mind in the next twenty-four hours...how much of it would be worth rereading? If your mind is anything like mine, very little!

When it comes to our partner, our mind is usually quick to judge and criticize—to point out all the ways in which they say or do the wrong thing. Or to take us back in time and replay all those old quarrels and grievances; relive all those times we were hurt or let down; open up old wounds and rub salt in them; and remind us that the good old days are over. Or it may pull us into the future and show us how bad life will be if we stay in this relationship (or how good it will be if we leave).

None of this is a problem if you know how to handle your mind effectively; the problem is, most of us don't. Our default is to get trapped inside-the-mind: we give it all our attention, take it very seriously, believe the things it says to us, and obey what it tells us to do. When you're inside-the-mind, you get lost in the smog of your own thought processes. And the thicker this smog becomes, the more your partner becomes a blur until you can barely see them through all your own judgments, criticisms, and grievances.

Inside-the-mind, you're both disconnected and reactive. You can't connect with your partner because you're too entangled in your own thoughts. And you can't respond to them effectively because you're on autopilot, reacting impulsively. Not surprisingly, this creates huge issues.

Neglecting Values

Values are our heart's deepest desires for how we want to behave; how we want to treat ourselves, others, and the world around us. In terms of your relationship, values describe the sort of partner you genuinely want to be. My clients often say they'd like to be more loving, kind, caring, generous, compassionate, supportive, fun-loving, easygoing, honest, fair, reliable, responsible, understanding, affectionate, and so on. These "desired qualities of behavior" are called values. In contrast, I've never heard clients say they'd like to be aggressive, hostile, sulky, nagging, moody, argumentative, threatening, uncaring, judgmental, critical, unforgiving, cold, punitive, or distant.

So consider this: When problems arise in your relationship, and difficult thoughts and feelings show up, how does your behavior change? Usually, when we're upset or angry, our values fly out of the window—and instead of behaving like the partner we want to be, we disconnect, react, avoid, or go inside-the-mind.

Both Partners Contribute

So there you have the five DRAIN processes: disconnection, reactivity, avoidance, inside-the-mind, and neglecting values. These patterns of behavior not only cause most relationship problems, but also make it hard to resolve them.

For example, people often describe their problems like this: "I want X but my partner wants Y," or "My partner keeps doing A, but I want them to do B," or "Whenever I do Q, my partner does R," or "My partner believes G, but I believe H." In other words, they see their problems primarily in terms of conflicting needs, desires, goals, or beliefs. However, this is rarely the case. Differences such as these are normal and natural, and common in all relationships—and with good communication and negotiation skills (which we'll cover later) they can often be peacefully resolved. But DRAIN prevents this from happening.

Now obviously, there are exceptions. Sometimes differences are truly irreconcilable. But even then, DRAIN massively amplifies the pain around these issues and makes them hard to discuss; we'll never know what's possible if we can't effectively communicate and negotiate with each other.

But what if your problem is something like this: "My partner did DEF and it really hurt me and I can't get over it"? Well, one thing's for sure: it's not easy to heal from major hurts. But (as we'll explore later), healing, forgiving, and repairing *are* possible; again, what prevents this is DRAIN.

For example, it's hard to address an issue if one partner is avoiding it—and impossible if both are. And even if we're not avoiding it, we can't talk it through calmly or cooperate on resolving it if one or both partners are disconnected, reactive, avoidant, inside-the-mind, or neglecting their values.

So as you work through this book, keep an eye out for the ways in which *both you and your partner* DRAIN the relationship. That's right: *you and your partner*. Both partners contribute to the problems in a relationship. Perhaps not equally, but both play a role in maintaining the ongoing issues.

Your mind may lodge an objection at this point, because most of us are quick to see our partner's faults, but often somewhat blind to our own. And when confronted with *our own* DRAIN behaviors, we're often quick to justify them ("I wouldn't do this if you didn't do that!"), deny them ("I don't do that!"), or downplay them ("It's not that bad. You're exaggerating!"). So we need to be painfully honest with ourselves. If you truly can't see any way that you contribute to the difficulties in your relationship, that's a huge problem; it indicates either a lack of self-awareness or an inability to be honest with yourself—and I recommend you talk it through with a therapist. Remember, there's no such thing as "the perfect partner"; both parties contribute to the difficulties.

And just as you aren't perfect, neither is your partner. So if you're blaming yourself for everything and portraying your partner as a saint, that's both unrealistic and unhealthy.

But what if your partner sees themselves as perfect? If they deny that they play any role in your relationship problems; if they claim that everything is "your fault," that all the issues start with you, that you are the only one who needs to change? If so, that's a big red flag, best addressed as discussed in chapter 2.

Of course, both partners also contribute *positively* to the relationship, and it's important to appreciate this. Therefore, in part 3 of the book, I'll encourage you to notice positive contributions—from both yourself and your partner—and appreciate the effect they have on your relationship. However, at this point, we're focusing on the negative.

To help you develop more self-awareness, I'm about to ask you to fill in a DRAIN worksheet. If you go to the free resources page on my website, thehappinesstrap.com, you can download a free e-book, called "ACT with Love: Extra Bits." This contains many useful free materials, such as worksheets and audio recordings. So I encourage you to download the e-book now, and scroll down to chapter 3, where you'll find a DRAIN worksheet with instructions. Alternatively, pull out a journal and jot a few notes about DRAIN in your relationship. First, write about your own DRAIN. After that, if you want to (it's not essential), you can also write about your partner's DRAIN.

Exercises to Do with Your Partner

In many chapters from here on, there's a section called *If Your Partner Is Willing*, containing exercises to do with your partner. Note the word "willing." There's no point doing these exercises grudgingly, resentfully, or half-heartedly. Unless you're both genuinely willing to do them, to build a better relationship, they'll flop or backfire.

These exercises are an opportunity for you both to have a good honest look at your relationship and how you can cooperate to improve it. Do them without any blaming, judgment, or criticism. And if any exercise turns into an argument, stop immediately. Take a break and reconvene later—but only when you're both genuinely willing.

When you discuss these exercises, it's often beneficial to go for a walk in the park or go out for a coffee or a drink. The different setting makes it easier for you to listen to each other without reacting negatively. Following is the first of these exercises.

If Your Partner Is Willing

The purpose of this exercise is for each of you to look honestly at how you DRAIN your relationship.

EXERCISE: Sharing Your DRAIN Worksheet

- Both fill in a DRAIN worksheet, as described earlier.

- Put aside some time (ideally twenty minutes) to share your worksheets and talk openly and honestly about it. Only share what you have written about *yourself.* Do not share what you've written about your partner's DRAIN, as it could trigger an argument.

- You may want to share what you learned about yourself from doing this. Did anything surprise you? Is there anything you regret?

- When your partner shares, do *not* mention things you think they should have added. Keep such thoughts to yourself, to prevent any argument. Instead, use this as an opportunity to learn about how your partner sees things, and to let them learn the same about you.

- Finish the exercise by thanking each other for sharing and listening.

Well, that brings us to the end of the chapter, and hopefully you can see how the DRAIN processes cause, maintain, or exacerbate many relationship problems. They have such a negative impact, it's hardly surprising that…

CHAPTER 4

You're Both Hurting

Ever seen a movie where the hero gets punched right in the face? A gruesome slow-mo close-up, where a spray of sweat and blood flies through the air? Notice how you wince, or flinch, or turn away even though you know it's only a movie? How ironic is it that we so easily relate to the nonexistent pain of a fictional movie character, but we often completely forget about the very real pain of the people we love?

Humans are social animals. We want to be loved, respected, and cared for. We want to get along with others, have a good time with them. When we fight with, reject, or withdraw from the people we love, we don't feel good. And nor do they. When there's conflict and tension in any relationship, both parties get hurt.

Your partner may not reveal their pain to you; they may just snap, or sulk, or storm out of the house, or quietly switch on the TV and start drinking—but deep inside, they're hurting, just like you. Your partner may refuse to talk to you, criticize you in scathing tones, or go out on the town with their friends, but deep inside, they're hurting, just like you. It is so important to remember this. We tend to get so caught up in our own pain, we easily forget our partner suffers too.

Suppose your partner has deep-seated fears of abandonment: afraid that you will leave them for someone "better." Or suppose they fear becoming trapped, controlled, or "smothered." When you fight, these fears will well up inside them; and they may not even be aware of such fear because it's buried under blame, anger, or resentment. Or suppose deep inside your partner feels unworthy: as if they're inadequate, unlovable, not good enough. This is painful in itself, but to make matters worse, when people feel this way, they often act in ways that strain the relationship. Your partner may continually seek approval, demand recognition for what they achieve or contribute, seek reassurance that you love or admire them, or become jealous and possessive. If you then react with frustration, scorn, criticism, impatience, or boredom, you will reinforce that deep-seated sense of unworthiness, which gives rise to even more pain.

What Was Your Relationship Like Before?

When I work with couples, in the first session I say: "Obviously you've come here to talk about the issues in your relationship and how we can resolve them, but before we get into that, I'd like to know what your relationship was like before the problems started." I then ask them each to answer the following questions:

- How did you first meet?

- Aside from their looks, what did you find most attractive about your partner? What personal qualities did you admire?

- What did you enjoy doing together? What did your partner say and do that made those times enjoyable?

- Describe one of the most enjoyable days you've ever spent together. Where were you? What did you do? How did you treat each other?

- What do you miss most about the "good old days" of your relationship?

- What do you see as your partner's greatest strengths and qualities?

There's a deliberate strategy here. Usually, both partners are frustrated, sad, and angry. Consumed by thoughts about what is wrong with the other. Hurting so much, they've forgotten what brought them together in the first place. And as they answer the questions, it connects them with warmer thoughts and feelings and memories. The tension lifts. Jaws unclench.

Frowns disappear. Faces soften. They settle into their chairs. Instead of glaring at each other or deliberately turning away, they start to look at each other and listen. One or both may even smile or tear up. It's heartwarming to see them rediscover a sense of connection.

Alas, it doesn't always happen like that. Sometimes one partner answers in an unhelpful manner: "I can't remember," "I don't know if we ever did enjoy being together," or "Even on our wedding day we were fighting." At other times, one partner is talking warmly and fondly, but the other is staring off into space, completely disinterested, or sneering, or looking bored. So these simple questions, and their answers, provide a wealth of information about the current state of the relationship.

Now take a moment to answer these questions yourself. Ponder them carefully. Better still, go to the free resources page on thehappinesstrap. com, download "ACT with Love: Extra Bits," and fill in the worksheet for this chapter (or alternatively, write in your journal). And as you do so, notice what thoughts and feelings arise:

- Can you contact any sense of warmth or appreciation for your partner?

- When you acknowledge their strengths and positive qualities, do you see them differently?

- Is it hard to acknowledge their positive attributes because you're so focused on what's wrong?

If you can't get in touch with any sense of warmth, tenderness, or appreciation for your partner, then you're probably in a great deal of pain, with your love buried under layers of resentment, hurt, anger, fear, or disappointment. If so, don't give yourself a hard time. Beating yourself up will only add to the pain that's already there. Instead, take a moment to acknowledge that you are hurting. And tell yourself something kind and caring—the sort of thing you might say to a friend if they were in as much pain as you are.

On the other hand, if this exercise does reconnect you with some warmth and tenderness for your partner, then notice how that feels. What's it like to look at your partner in this way, instead of as "a problem to be fixed"?

Moving On

The next thing I do in that first session is to ask each partner why they came, what they hope to achieve, and what they see as the main issue(s) with their relationship. I ask them to describe the issues as nonjudgmentally as possible—for example, instead of saying "He's a lazy slob," try saying "I have much higher standards of cleanliness than he does." This is an important first step: to start using factual descriptions instead of harsh judgments. And it doesn't come naturally for most of us. All too often, I'll have to intervene. What follows is an example from my first session with Juan and Claire. (Note: I've changed the names and certain details of everyone I describe in this book, in order to protect their identity.)

Juan: She's such a nag.

Russ: What do you mean by that?

Juan: She's always on my back. Do this. Do that. Do the other.

Russ: What's she asking you to do?

Juan: Clean up mostly. Pick up and clean up. That sort of shit.

Russ: So Claire often asks you repeatedly to pick up and clean up?

Juan: You bet she does.

Notice how I prompt Juan to move away from a harsh, negative judgment of her personality—"She's a nag"—to a nonjudgmental description of her behavior—"So Claire often asks you repeatedly to pick up and clean up?" Nonjudgmental describing is an important skill to develop. Why? Well, would you like to be described in harsh judgmental terms—such as bitch, nag, slob, lazy, dumb, selfish, mean, loser, useless—that assassinate your character? The more you see your partner through the filter of harsh negative judgments, the more you lose touch with who they really are. The person you once admired disappears behind a wall of condemnation. So you'll reap great rewards if you make your descriptions less judgmental.

On a separate but related note: while one partner speaks, I ask the other one to listen very attentively. I say, "It's hard to listen under these circumstances because no one likes to get negative feedback. And if you're anything like most human beings, you'll want to butt in and object or defend yourself or put your own viewpoint across or strike back with complaints of your own. However, you're probably well aware that responding that way is not very effective, right?" They usually answer yes, but if they're uncertain, I ask, "What normally happens when you respond in those ways?" The answer is usually: "We keep fighting and nothing gets resolved."

"So," I say, "how about looking at this as an opportunity to learn a new way of responding to your partner: to pay attention with an attitude of openness and curiosity instead of hostility or boredom?" Attentive listening and nonjudgmental describing both help to create a safe space, where both partners can open up and talk more freely about their difficulties. And as each partner tells their story, I repeatedly ask questions like: "So when she speaks to you that way, how do you feel?" or "What feelings show up for you when he doesn't follow through on what he says?" or "How do you feel when they storm out of the room like that?" I do this to help them recognize *they are both hurting*. For example, here's a bit more of Juan and Claire:

Russ:	So when Juan calls you a "nag" or a "bitch," how do you feel?
Claire:	Furious.
Russ:	Furious?
Claire:	Yes! He's got no right to talk to me that way. (*Her face flushes, her arms are crossed, her voice is loud. She glares at Juan, who looks down at his feet.*)
Russ:	I'm just wondering, Claire, almost always when someone is furious or angry, if we dig a bit deeper, we usually find something underneath the anger. Usually something quite painful. And I wonder if you could just check in with yourself and see if this might be the case for you. Just see if you can take a few deep breaths and kind of breathe into that anger—and see if there's

another feeling, a more painful feeling, lying underneath it.

Claire: *(eyes tearing, voice wavering)* I feel like he hates me.

Russ: And what is that like? To feel like the person you love hates you?

Claire: It's awful.

Russ: *(turning to Juan)* Juan, is that what you want Claire to feel?

Juan: No way. *(Shaking his head vigorously.)* No way. *(He gulps heavily, his face softens, and his eyes tear up. He looks at Claire and speaks very softly, his voice cracking.)* Of course I don't hate you. I love you.

So what just happened? Claire dared to be open and vulnerable, and share some of her painful feelings with Juan. This is radically different from her usual response. Usually she shows Juan her angry, judgmental exterior. In return, he becomes defensive and critical. Claire then becomes even angrier, and a vicious cycle ensues. But when Claire opens up and lets Juan see how much she is hurting, he responds very differently. He sees her pain, and wants to help ease it. Instead of lashing out or withdrawing, he reaches out to comfort her.

Trapped inside-the-mind, we forget our partner is hurting. We get hooked by anger, resentment, and self-righteousness, wrapped up in thoughts like: *It's all too hard. It shouldn't be this difficult! Why won't they get off my case?* We become so focused on what is wrong with our partner, or so upset at the way they have treated us, we forget they are a human being with feelings. We need to remember that, just like us, they came into this relationship wanting to love and be loved, to care and be cared for, to enrich their life by sharing it with another.

No one enters a relationship because they want to fight, quarrel, bicker, blame, judge, hurt, reject, or withdraw. So when we're hurting badly, our partners are likely hurting too. When we recognize that we're both in the same boat, it's easier to respond with kindness, caring, and understanding (rather than hostility or rejection, which is obviously much worse for your relationship).

So here's another brief exercise. First, if you haven't yet done so, go to the free resources page on thehappinesstrap.com, and download the free e-book, "ACT with Love: Extra Bits." Scroll down to chapter 4, and you'll find a worksheet to guide you through the exercise. (Alternatively, write in your journal.)

EXERCISE: You're Both Hurting

1. Take a few minutes to write about the major issues in your relationship—with nonjudgmental description, instead of judgment and criticism. For example, "Greg rarely helps with the housework" instead of "Greg is a lazy bastard." This is difficult to do at first, so go easy on yourself. And if a harsh judgment slips through, as soon as you notice it, silently say, "Aha! A judgment!" or "There's judging!" Then cross it out and write something nonjudgmental instead.

2. Write about the painful emotions you have experienced because of these issues. What painful thoughts and feelings have you struggled with? If the main feelings you notice are anger, fury, resentment, rage, or frustration, see if you can "go deeper." Beneath the surface of anger, you will usually find sadness, guilt, shame, fear, rejection, loneliness, inadequacy, anxiety, hopelessness—or an intensely painful sense of feeling unloved, unwanted, unappreciated.

3. Acknowledge to yourself, openly and honestly, that this relationship has been painful. You have suffered. It has not been easy. You came into it with all sorts of expectations, many of which have not been met. You had all sorts of dreams for the future, many of which have failed to materialize. You had all sorts of illusions about who your partner is, many of which have been shattered. Given what you have been through, it's completely natural to feel the way you do.

4. Now this is the most challenging part (and if you're not willing to do it, that's okay). Take a few minutes to reflect on how your partner has also suffered. They may never have spoken about this to you—especially if they're not very good at talking about their feelings. If so, use your imagination: What must it be like for your partner to be on the receiving end of your DRAIN? If they tend to cut off, go quiet, and withdraw, what must that be like— hiding away and closing down in order to cope? If they tend to brood, dwell, and rehash the past, how painful must that be— suffering again and again by replaying old events that can never be undone? If they snap or yell, consider: How unpleasant must that feel, to be full of such anger or resentment? (Surely there's no joy or pleasure involved.)

Many people find step 4 confronting or uncomfortable, and are naturally reluctant to do it. Especially if they have thoughts like: *So what if they're hurting? They deserve it. Why should I care?* The thing is, if you *can* acknowledge you're both hurting, it will help you move from tension and conflict to resolution and repair. Why? Because after this acknowledgment, it's easier to tap into a sense of kindness, caring, and understanding—which are all essential ingredients for restoring vitality and love. However, if you're not willing or able to do this right now, then skip it; come back to it later when you're ready. (As you work through more of the book, it will get easier to do.)

If Your Partner is Willing

This exercise is to help you both acknowledge how you're hurting.

EXERCISE: Sharing Your Pain

1. Each individually work through the four steps outlined earlier. Once completed, read each other your responses to steps 1 and

2. (Step 3 is intended just for yourself; it's not for sharing. And step 4 comes later.)

2. As your partner speaks about their responses (to steps 1 and 2), practice "engaging." In other words, pay full attention, with an attitude of curiosity and openness. Notice your partner's tone of voice, the expressions on their face, their body language, and their choice of words. Be genuinely curious about the thoughts, feelings, or attitudes they reveal. If you notice the urge to interrupt or defend or "counterattack," don't act on it. Instead, listen as if one of your all-time heroes is giving an important speech. Engaging fully is one of the greatest gifts you can give your partner. It powerfully sends the message, "I care about you. You matter to me." (Check your own experience. How do you feel when someone pays attention to you in this manner: Important? Valued? Respected? Seen and heard?)

3. Finally discuss step 4 and see how accurately you guessed your partner's feelings. You may be surprised—either by how accurate you are or by how far you've missed the mark.

In part 1 of the book, we looked at common love myths, considered what's within your control, and explored three options for responding to problematic relationships. In part 2, we looked at how DRAIN (disconnection, reactivity, avoidance, inside-the-mind, neglecting values) causes, maintains, and exacerbates common relationship problems, and we confronted the reality that both partners get hurt. Now it's time for part 3: getting active.

Part III

Getting Active

CHAPTER 5

The Choice Point

"Can you please fix my partner?"

When people first go to couples counseling, this is often their agenda. And naturally so. By the time they reach the point of seeing a counselor, both parties are hurting badly, and both desperately want each other to change; to stop doing things that hurt, and start doing things that heal, repair, and rebuild. And obviously, the best results occur when *both you and your partner* willingly work at this; however, it's sensible to start by focusing *on your own behavior*, because that's where you have most control. I know I've said this before, but it bears repeating: the more control you have over *your* behavior, the more effectively you can influence your partner's.

When I say this, some folks get angry: "Are you saying it's my fault?" "Are you saying that I'm to blame?" "Why should I have to work on myself when they're the problem?" I calmly reply that I'm not saying any of those things; I'm not finding fault or attributing blame. I'm purely being pragmatic. If you want to heal the wounds, move on from the past, resolve the problems, and build a loving relationship...the most effective place to start is by working on your own behavior. And as you change your own behavior for the better, you'll notice your partner's behavior improving too.

Other folks get a bit anxious: "But what if I do all the work and they do nothing?" "What if they take advantage of me?" "What if their behavior gets worse?" I calmly explain that such outcomes are unlikely, and even if they occur, you'll learn how to handle them. But...if you want to handle them effectively, in ways that are healthy for your relationship, you'll need good control over what you say and do.

For example, some people tend to put the needs of others ahead of their own; and instead of standing up for themselves, they allow others to walk all over them (like the proverbial "doormat"). Psychologists call this "being passive." The greater your passivity in a relationship, the more likely you are to feel tired, run-down, stressed, burned-out, anxious, neglected, mistreated, or "taken advantage of." And that, in turn, often breeds resentment. In the long run, passivity will take its toll on both you and your partner.

The opposite of being passive is "being aggressive." Aggression means standing up for yourself and taking care of your needs in a way that's uncaring and disrespectful of others: instead of a doormat, you're a battering ram. We all know what it's like to be on the receiving end of aggression: to have someone yelling, snapping, judging, blaming, criticizing, threatening, or insulting us. Pretty awful, right? Aggression rapidly sucks the life from a relationship.

Many of us swing between passivity and aggression, instead of choosing the healthy third option: "being assertive." Assertiveness means standing up for your rights and taking care of your needs in a way that is considerate, fair, and caring—for *both yourself and the other person involved*. It's a healthy, constructive way to look after yourself and get your needs met in your relationship, because you practice self-respect and self-care while simultaneously being considerate, fair, and caring toward your partner. We'll explore assertiveness in chapter 15; for now I simply want to emphasize: if you wish to be assertive (rather than passive or aggressive), you need control over what *you* say and do.

So as a first step toward greater self-control, let's look at a simple tool, which I co-created with my colleagues, Joe Ciarrochi and Ann Bailey. It's called...

The Choice Point

"The choice point" is a concept that helps us understand our own behavior and the effects it has upon our life. We can represent this concept as a diagram, as illustrated. You'll note there are two arrows, labeled "toward" and "away."

When we behave like the sort of person we truly want to be and do things that enhance and enrich our life, we call these behaviors "toward moves"; they take us *toward* the person we want to be and the life we want to build.

When we behave *unlike* the person we want to be, and do things that make our life worse, we call these "away moves"; they take us *away* from the person we want to be and the life we want to build.

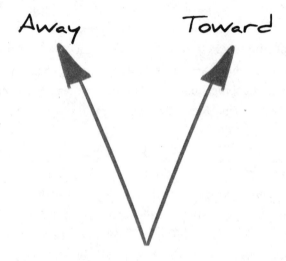

In chapter 3, you identified your own DRAIN (disconnection, reactivity, avoidance, inside-the-mind, neglecting values). I'm guessing your list included at least some of the following: sulking, withdrawing, storming off, complaining, snapping, lashing out, making hurtful comments or nasty remarks, threatening, judging, criticizing, losing your temper. Now do you consider those behaviors to be toward moves—behaving like the person you really want to be, doing things that enrich and enhance your life—or do you see them as the opposite: away moves?

Now in the next diagram, you'll see at the bottom "situations, thoughts, and feelings." This refers to the fact that all day long, our thoughts and feelings and the situations we're in keep changing. And when we're feeling reasonably good, and the situation we're in is not too challenging, it's relatively easy to choose those toward moves: to behave like the person we want to be and do things that improve our life.

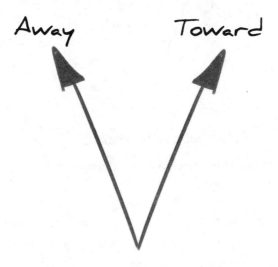

Away   Toward

Situation(s),
Thoughts, & Feelings

Unfortunately, when difficult thoughts and feelings show up—especially strong emotions like anger, anxiety, and sadness—we easily get "hooked" by them, like a fish on the end of a line. Those thoughts and feelings hook us, and reel us in, and jerk us around, and pull us into doing away moves. For example, when anger hooks us, it typically pulls us into snapping, yelling, insulting, or harshly criticizing. You can see this, following.

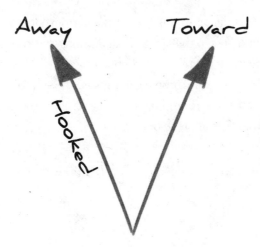

Fortunately, there are times when we're able to "unhook" ourselves from difficult thoughts and feelings. This enables us to interrupt our away moves, and choose toward moves instead.

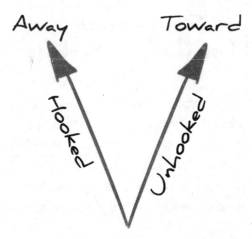

The greater our ability to unhook from difficult thoughts and feelings, and choose toward moves over away moves, the greater our chances of building a healthy relationship. So that's basically what the rest of the book involves. You'll first develop unhooking skills, and use them to take the power and impact out of all your difficult thoughts and feelings, so they can't keep jerking you around. Then you'll ramp up your ability to choose toward moves by a) exploring your values and using them as a guide for how you behave; and b) learning new skills to *constructively* influence your partner's behavior, in ways that are healthy for the relationship.

As you do this, you'll see for yourself what I said earlier: when you change your own behavior for the better, you'll notice your partner's behavior improving too. There are several reasons for this:

1. As you cut down on your own away moves, your partner's likely to feel better and have a more positive attitude toward you. For example, if you do less judging, criticizing, blaming, or snapping, your partner's bound to feel less defensive or resentful, and therefore more amenable to talking things through and cooperating.

2. As you choose more toward moves, that breathes new life into the relationship and reduces tension and conflict. And the less tension and conflict, the less your partner will hurt, which in turn makes them less likely to do away moves.

3. As you use new skills to constructively influence your partner's behavior, you're likely to get much better results (as opposed to those destructive things you say and do when hooked).

Why am I emphasizing these points? Because one of the biggest barriers to improving any relationship is focusing on what's *out of* your control. The more you focus on what's *within* your control—what you say and do, and how you say and do it—the better your chances of building the relationship you want. That's why it's so important to…

Know Your Values

Earlier, I described values as *our heart's deepest desires for how we want to behave; how we want to treat ourselves, others, and the world around us.* We'll explore this in more depth shortly. First, let's consider why it's useful to connect with our values:

- They can help us make better choices, especially in the face of great challenges.

- They're like an inner compass that can guide us and help us find our way.

- They bring a sense of meaning and purpose to what we do.

- They provide motivation, giving us the strength to do what really matters.

- When we translate them into action, they give us a sense of fulfillment—a sense of being true to ourselves, more like the sort of person we really want to be.

Many people confuse values with goals, but they're radically different concepts. A value is a quality we desire to bring to our behavior, a quality that guides our words and actions. In contrast, a goal describes what we want to have, get, or achieve. So if you want to "find a partner" or "get married" or "have children," those are all goals. But if you want to "be loving," that's a value. And notice that you can live the value of being loving—that is, you can bring a loving quality to your words and actions—even if you don't achieve the goals of finding a partner, or getting married, or having children; you can still be loving toward yourself, your friends, your family, your dog, and so on.

Here are some more examples:

- You aim to get respect, love, or understanding from someone else: *goal.*

- You aim to be respectful, loving, or understanding and to bring these qualities to your words and actions: *values.*

- You aim to have a child: *goal.*

- You aim to be loving, kind, and supportive in your closest relationships (whether you have a child or not): *values*.

- You aim to go traveling overseas: *goal*.

- You aim to be curious, open, and appreciative while you are traveling (even if you're just strolling around your neighborhood): *values*.

- You aim to buy a house: *goal*.

- You aim to be supportive, caring, and protective of your family (even if you don't have a house): *values*.

Notice that in each example you can live by your values, whether you achieve the goal or not. So if you want to become rich or famous, or have a great body, or get your partner to stop that annoying habit, or upgrade your car, or live somewhere else, or make your kids listen to you...those are all goals. They're all things you're trying to get, have, or achieve.

In contrast, values describe how you want to treat yourself, others, and the world around you; they're the qualities you want to bring to your ongoing actions, both now and in the future—as you pursue your goals, when you achieve your goals, and even when you *don't* achieve your goals.

Emotional Goals

Most of us want to feel cherished, supported, nurtured, respected, important, appreciated, relaxed, happy, content, passionate, "in love," and so on. Technically, these are known as "emotional goals." An emotional goal describes how we want to *feel*, whereas a value describes how we want to *behave*. It's natural to want pleasant feelings; the problem is, we have very little control over whether we get them or not.

Values are far more empowering than emotional goals, because regardless of how we are feeling, our values are always accessible—as long as we know what they are. Most of us are somewhat vague about our values, so to help you clarify and connect with them, let's do some exercises.

EXERCISE: Connect and Reflect

The "connect and reflect" exercise is a good way to get in touch with your core values. Part A involves recalling a pleasant memory. Part B involves reflecting on what you said or did in the memory. (And if you'd like my voice to guide you through this, download "ACT with Love: Extra Bits" from the free resources page on thehappinesstrap.com, and in chapter 5 you'll find an audio recording.)

Part A

Recall a pleasant memory (recent or distant) that involves you and your partner having a good time, doing some activity you both enjoy, and getting on well with each other as you do it. This might involve playing a sport, hiking, swimming, going out for dinner, having a chat, going for a drive, hugging and kissing, sunbathing on the beach, playing with the dog or the kids, having sex…any enjoyable activity.

Now make this memory as vivid as possible. Relive it as if it's happening here and now. Sense it, feel it, recreate it. Where are you? What are you doing? What can you see, hear, touch, taste, or smell? (If you can't clearly visualize it, that's not a problem; just get a sense of what's going on.)

What does your partner look like? How are they dressed? What are they saying or doing? What's their tone of voice, the expression on their face, their body posture?

Tap into the emotion: What does it feel like to be getting on well with your partner, doing something you both enjoy? Let yourself really feel it.

Appreciate it. Drink it in. Savor it.

Please do this for at least a minute, before moving on.

Part B

Now look at the memory as if it's on a TV screen. (If you can't visualize it, no problem. Just get a sense of studying or examining the memory.)

Now focus on yourself inside that memory. What are you saying and doing? How are you treating your partner? How are you responding to them? For example, are you being warm, open, loving, kind, fun-loving, playful, lighthearted, connected, engaged, interested, appreciative, honest, respectful, real, open, curious, courageous, intimate, sensual, creative, enthusiastic, affectionate, humorous, adventurous?

Consider this for at least one minute, and come up with four or five words to describe the qualities of your behavior.

Part C

Now do this again with a different memory. This time, remember an occasion when your partner was hurting, struggling, or suffering in some way, and you responded to their pain like the sort of person you really want to be. First recall the memory, making it as vivid as possible. Then zoom in on yourself in the memory, noticing what you're saying and doing, and come up with several words to describe the qualities of your actions. For example, are you being kind, caring, understanding, respectful, compassionate, supportive, helpful, reliable, responsible, protective, courageous, connected, engaged?

The words you came up with in the previous exercises are likely to reflect your values as a partner: qualities you want to bring to your words and actions. You can think of values as a kind of magical glue that binds together the tiniest little action to the biggest long-term goal. If your value is "being caring," that glues together everything from making your partner a coffee, to listening to them attentively, to holding their hand as they lie in a hospital bed. If your value is "being supportive," that glues together everything from sharing the housework, to paying off a mortgage together, to helping your partner change careers.

EXERCISE: A Values Checklist

There are no such things as "right" or "wrong" values. It's like ice cream. My favorite flavor is maple walnut; my son's is chocolate. That doesn't mean my flavor is "right" and his is "wrong"—or vice versa. We each like what we like. Similarly, your values are your values, and you don't need to defend or justify them. Following is a list of common relationship values. They are not the "right" or "best" ones—they're just common. So please read through them, and alongside each value write a letter. If it's a very important value for you, write V; if quite important, write Q; if not important, write N. (If you prefer not to write in the book, use the list provided in chapter 5 of "ACT with Love: Extra Bits," at thehappinesstrap.com.)

In this relationship, I want to be...

1. ____ Accepting: allowing my partner to be who they are, without judging or criticizing them

2. ____ Affectionate: saying and doing things with fondness and tenderness

3. ____ Assertive: calmly, fairly, and considerately standing up for my rights, asking for what I want, and saying no to what I don't want

4. ____ Attentive: being present and engaged with my partner, giving them my full attention

5. ____ Authentic: being genuine and real, showing my true self

6. ____ Caring/self-caring: actively taking care of my partner and myself

7. ____ Compassionate/self-compassionate: acknowledging pain —in my partner or myself—and responding with genuine kindness

8. ____ Cooperative: being willing to assist and work with my partner

9. ____ Courageous: being brave or bold; persisting in the face of fear or risk

10. ____ Creative: being imaginative, inventive, or innovative

11. ____ Curious: being open-minded and interested; being willing to explore and discover

12. ____ Expressive: conveying my thoughts and feelings through what I say and do

13. ____ Fair/just: acting with fairness and justice—toward myself and my partner

14. ____ Flexible: being willing and able to adjust and adapt to changing circumstances

15. ____ Forgiving/self-forgiving: letting go of resentments and grudges toward my partner and myself

16. ____ Friendly: being warm, open, caring, and agreeable

17. ____ Grateful: being appreciative for what I have received

18. ____ Helpful: giving, helping, contributing, assisting, or sharing

19. ____ Honest: being honest, truthful, and sincere—with myself and my partner

20. ____ Independent/autonomous: choosing for myself how I live and what I do

21. ____ Kind: being considerate, helpful, or caring—to myself and my partner

22. ____ Loving: saying and doing things lovingly, with great care

23. ____ Loyal: being firm and consistent in my support for and allegiance with my partner

24. ____ Open: revealing myself, letting my partner know my thoughts and feelings, and encouraging and allowing my partner to do likewise

25. ____ Persistent/committed: being willing to continue, despite problems or difficulties

26. ____ Playful: being humorous, fun-loving, lighthearted

27. ____ Protective/self-protective: looking after the safety and security of my partner or myself

28. ____ Respectful/self-respectful: treating my partner or myself with care, fairness, and consideration

29. ____ Responsible: being trustworthy, reliable, and accountable for my actions

30. ____ Sensual: giving, expressing, or appreciating physical pleasure, through the five senses

31. ____ Sexual: accepting and expressing my erotic thoughts, feelings, drives, and desires

32. ____ Supportive/self-supportive: being helpful, encouraging, and available—to my partner and myself

33. ____ Trusting: willing to believe in the honesty, reliability, responsibility, or competence of my partner or myself

34. ____ Trustworthy: being loyal, honest, faithful, sincere, responsible, and reliable

35. ____ Understanding: being aware of and open to my partner's feelings, perspectives, and opinions

36. Other: _____

37. Other: _____

38. Other: _____

_____

Hopefully you're now a lot clearer on your values. But just for good measure, let's do one last exercise.

_____

Exercise: One Year from Now

Imagine that it's one year from now, and magic has happened. Both you and your partner have healed your wounds, resolved your issues, and built a fantastic relationship. And I take your partner aside, and I interview them. I ask them about what you stand for in the relationship, and the role that you have played in their life, and what they think are your five greatest qualities as a partner.

Now imagine your partner replying to my questions; imagine them saying whatever it is, deep in your heart, you would most like to hear. (Remember, magic has happened! This is not about what your partner would realistically say; it's a fantasy. In a world where magic could happen and dreams could come true, what you would *love* to hear them say?) Imagine them describing your character, your strengths, and your greatest qualities as a partner.

Close your eyes, or fix on a spot, and take a couple of minutes to imagine this as vividly as possible. Let yourself daydream: What would you *love* to hear your partner say?

The qualities you wanted your partner to mention are values: desired qualities of behavior. And if the same values kept cropping up in all the previous exercises, they are likely your "core values" (i.e., very important ones).

This is golden information because our values provide the bedrock for lasting love; neglect them and your relationship crumbles like a house without a foundation.

And keep in mind, values are a two-way street: you apply them to yourself *and* your partner. So suppose you identified values like being kind, caring, and supportive; the aim is to treat yourself in these ways, as well as your partner, so both of you reap the rewards.

What About "Needs"?

Needs are things we require on an ongoing basis to survive and thrive. Unlike a goal, a need can't be ticked off a list: done, achieved, completed. A need is ongoing. For example, while each person's needs are unique (and there's no list of the "right" or "best" ones), here are some relationship needs that many of us have: *affection, intimacy, trust, kindness, caring, understanding, security, respect, honesty, support, sharing, connection, love, acceptance, autonomy.*

In other words, these are things we want from our partner, on an ongoing basis. And every time we set out to meet a need, that's a goal. For example, we *need* to eat food to survive. So every time we set out to eat something, that's a goal. And when we eat it, that goal is achieved. And the *need* to eat is temporarily satisfied. But "temporarily" is the key word, here. A need can never be *permanently* satisfied: it gives rise to recurrent goals, throughout one's life.

So a need describes something we continually pursue throughout our life, but can never permanently achieve. For example, if our need is to have affection, or love, or respect, there's no way to *permanently* satisfy that need, to such an extent that we'll never want more. However, each need gives rise to a vast number of short-term, medium-term, and long-term goals, many of which *can* be achieved.

It's important to understand the difference between needs and values, so we can focus on what's most within our control. Here are some examples:

- To be kind (to self or others) = value

- To receive kindness from others = need

- To be respectful (to self or others) = value

- To get respect from others = need

- To be loving (to self or others) = value

- To be loved by others = need

- To be affectionate = values

- To have affection from others = need

Notice the huge and very important difference: values describe *how we want to behave* on an ongoing basis, whereas needs describe *what we want to get* on an ongoing basis. We have far more control over the former than the latter.

For example, let's suppose that "being respectful" is an important value; in other words, you want to behave respectfully; you want to say and do things that are respectful to yourself and others. Here are some possibilities for acting on that value:

- Treat yourself with respect.

- Treat others with respect.

- Assertively ask others to treat you with respect.

- Notice, appreciate, and thank others when they treat you with respect.

- Build relationships with people who think respect is important.

- Talk openly about why respect matters to you, and what you think it looks like and sounds like.

- Avoid interactions with people that don't treat you with respect.

- Model respectful behavior for others.

Note how these are all actions you can take in line with your value of being respectful; they are all *within your control*. You can do them even when you don't meet your need of getting respect from others. These values-guided actions all increase the *probability* you'll get respect. They don't guarantee it, but they do make it much more likely. (In later chapters, we'll look at how to get your needs met more effectively through acting in line with your values—and also what to do if, despite everything, your needs still aren't getting met.)

Now aside from goals and needs, there's one more concept that often gets confused with values, and that's…

Rules

Rules are often useful. We'd be in trouble if we didn't have rules about which side of the road to drive on, or how fast we can drive. But when we hold onto rules too tightly, we become inflexible in our behavior; and often, we can feel those rules restricting us: a sense of constraint, obligation, or burden.

In contrast, values are about "opening your heart," doing what's meaningful, and they give us a sense of lightness, openness, and freedom. Here are two examples to clarify the difference:

Value: Being kind

Rule: I *should always* be kind, no exceptions.

Value: Being supportive

Rule: I *have to always* put my partner's needs first.

A value can usually be expressed in one or two words (e.g., "loving" or "being loving," "kindness" or "being kind"), whereas a rule usually requires a whole sentence, and tells you what you can or can't do. (Rules are often easy to identify because they tend to include words like "should," "must," "have to," "ought," "don't," "won't," "right," "wrong," "shan't," "can't," "good," "bad," "always," "never," "can't unless," "shouldn't because," "won't until.")

This distinction between rules and values is important for at least three reasons. First, when you go through life bound by your rules, you feel limited, burdened, restricted, whereas living by your values brings lightness, freedom, and opportunity. Second, there are almost limitless ways of acting on any value, whereas a rule massively restricts what you can do. So living by your values gives you a huge amount of choice, whereas rules significantly narrow and limit your options. Third, when we hold on tightly to our rules—and insist that our rules are "right" and our partner's are "wrong"—this usually pulls us away from our values, and becomes a source of conflict.

For example: Heath spends long hours at work and often comes home late. Zoe thinks this is not good for the kids, and wants him to come home earlier to spend more quality time with the family. Heath says he has to work hard to earn good money to give his kids "the best in life." Zoe says he should come earlier because the kids need quality time with their father.

At first glance, it may appear like they have different values. But they're not actually talking about values at all. "Work hard," "earn money," "spend time with the kids": those are all "rules," not values. A rule tells you what you can or can't, should or shouldn't do; values describe the qualities you want to bring to your words and actions. Both Heath and Zoe want to do the best for their kids: provide for them, look after them, and help them to grow, develop, and thrive. They both have core values of being loving, being supportive, and being caring—and there are soooo many different ways they can act on those values.

So the problem here is not different values but different rules. Heath's rule is "work hard to buy the kids what they need." By following that rule, he earns good money to pay for family holidays, provide clothes and toys for his children, and give them a roof over their head. Zoe's rule is "spend time together as a family." If they follow that rule, they can bond, have quality time, and develop richer and healthier relationships.

If Heath and Zoe could recognize they share the same values, it would change things. From a place of shared values, they could step back and take a look at their rules. This would enable them to see how their rules, not their values, are creating conflict. They could then experiment with bending the rules, to accommodate both their needs. (We'll look at how to do this later in the book.)

So now that you know what values are, and how they differ from goals, needs, and rules, it's time to write a values statement. Please do this in your journal, or use the worksheet in "ACT with Love: Extra Bits." (And from now on, instead of giving the full name of the e-book, we'll shorten it to "Extra Bits.") Based on the previous exercises, list three to six values you want to actively bring into your relationship. Begin like this: *In this relationship, I want to be…*

After you've finished, read it through and consider: Does this sound more like the person you want to be? If the answer is yes, you're on the right track. If the answer is no, you're not yet in touch with your values, so please go back and work through the chapter again.

If Your Partner Is Willing

Both complete the exercises in this chapter. Then share your thoughts with each other. You may find your values are very similar, or you may discover significant differences. If the latter, don't make that a problem: "Oh no. We're so different! How are we ever going to make this work?" Recognize that these are simply "differences." It's not that you have the "right" values and your partner has the "wrong" ones, or vice versa; you're just different. In upcoming chapters, you'll see that even if these differences are huge, you can still have a healthy relationship.

Remember too, that what at first seem to be "different values" are often actually just different "rules," as in the example of Heath and Zoe. So if your values appear to differ greatly, see if you can dig a bit deeper and find common ground. This isn't always possible, but it usually is.

Putting Your Values into Play

I said earlier that our values are like a compass. We can use them for guidance to keep us on track, or to find our way again if we get lost. But a compass won't give us a journey; for that, we need to take action. So the next step is to translate your values into actions: use them to guide your toward moves.

Think about little things you could say and do, in line with your values statement, that are likely to enhance your relationship. (If you're so hurt, angry, or resentful toward your partner that you're not willing to start on this yet, that's okay. Leave it for now, and come back to it later when you're ready.)

Each morning, pick one or two values from your statement and look for opportunities to "sprinkle" them into your activities throughout the day. (You may pick the same values every day, or you may vary them; it doesn't matter.) For example, if you pick "caring," look for opportunities to say caring things, do caring things, or bring a caring quality to your words and gestures. Following are a few ideas to get you started.

Words. What can you say to your partner that shows them you care? This could be something like "I love you," "I'm here for you," "How can I support you?" or "I appreciate having you in my life." Even simple phrases such as "Thank you," "I'm sorry," or "Please forgive me" can go a long way if said genuinely. Consider text messages, cards, phone calls, videos, and e-mails as well as the spoken word.

Actions. What caring actions can you take? What might contribute positively to your partner's health, well-being, and vitality? This might include anything from cooking dinner, fixing the car, or organizing a night out, to helping your partner with chores or tasks, or giving small gifts. Caring actions may also include listening attentively to your partner, taking the time to understand their fears or frustrations, holding hands, and so on.

Yourself. Don't forget values are a two-way street. What caring words can you say to yourself? What caring things can you do for yourself?

As you do these things, write about them in your journal or use the worksheet in "Extra Bits."

- At the end of the day, write down which values you brought into play, what you said and did, and how it felt. Consider: What does it feel like to act like the partner you want to be? What effect does it have on your relationship?

- When you neglect your values (as we all do at times), notice what stopped you. What thoughts, feelings, memories, or urges hooked you?

It's Not All Sweetness and Roses

Values-guided actions are the lifeblood of any close relationship; without them, it shrivels up and dies. But a values-based life is not all bliss, joy, and happiness. Although it gives rise to many wonderful moments, it also involves facing your fears, tackling your problems, and dealing with obstacles and setbacks. So there will be highs *and* lows, pleasure *and* pain, sweetness *and* sorrow. (Remember the first line of chapter 1: "Love and pain are intimate dance partners; they go hand in hand.")

However, although at times it will bring discomfort, there are many benefits to living by our values. When we live in this way, we experience a sense of meaning, purpose, and vitality and the deep fulfillment that comes from being true to ourselves.

The problem is, it's often hard to truly live by our values, because we so easily get hooked by our thoughts and feelings. So that's what the next few chapters will address. In the meantime, sprinkle your values liberally into your relationship, and notice what it feels like to be the partner you want to be.

CHAPTER 6

Dropping Anchor

"Hell is other people," said the great philosopher Jean-Paul Sartre. But he was only half right. "Heaven is other people," too. Our deepest, closest relationships give rise to many different thoughts and feelings—some of them wonderful, some of them dreadful. The painful ones may include: contempt, anger, frustration, judgment, resentment, sadness, despair, disappointment, loneliness, hopelessness, anxiety, insecurity, sadness, distrust...and the list goes on, and on. But it's important to remember that all these thoughts and feelings are *normal*. They are normal, natural, human reactions when things don't go well in a relationship. When tension builds or conflict erupts, we can't expect to feel happy, content, or relaxed. The greater the gap between the relationship we want and the relationship we've got, the more difficult thoughts and feelings we'll have.

Habitual Modes of Responding to Pain

Of course, as your relationship improves, those difficult thoughts and feelings will show up less often. However, no relationship is perfect. Sooner or later, issues will arise, and those unpleasant inner experiences will return. But the *real* problem is not those thoughts and feelings. The *real* problem is that we have two habitual modes of responding to them: we either OBEY or we STRUGGLE.

In OBEY mode, our thoughts and feelings dominate us; they dictate our actions, push us around, tell us what we have to say and do. In STRUGGLE mode, we do whatever we can to avoid or get rid of our unwanted thoughts and feelings: fight with them, push them down, or do what we can to avoid them. And much of the time, we both OBEY and STRUGGLE simultaneously.

OBEY Mode

OBEY mode means exactly what it says: when difficult thoughts and feelings show up, you obey them. You allow them to control whatever you say and do; to push you around as if you are a robot with no conscious will. In OBEY mode, you become the "reactive partner." You're on autopilot, acting out mindlessly or impulsively. If anger shows up, you allow it to jerk you around like a puppet on a string; you may yell or lash out, say hurtful things, or storm out of the room and slam the door. If jealousy shows up, you may fly off the handle without any justification, start spying on your partner, or make unfair accusations. If fear shows up, you may allow it to command your every move: you hide away, avoid taking risks, or run away from your challenges.

When you go through life in OBEY mode, you end up doing many things you regret. You have little or no self-awareness, and tend to take action without much care or deliberation. As a result, you often act inconsistently with your own values.

STRUGGLE Mode

STRUGGLE mode means doing whatever we can to avoid or get rid of unwanted thoughts and feelings. There are four types of strategy we all use to do this: distraction, opting out, thinking strategies, and substances. Let's take a quick look at each.

Distraction. You distract yourself from unwanted thoughts and feelings through social media, TV, books, computer games, e-mail, surfing the Net, socializing, gambling, exercise, working hard, and so on.

Opting out. You opt out of situations where unpleasant thoughts and feelings arise. You may physically withdraw from your partner, go out of your way to avoid them, avoid raising or discussing painful issues, or avoid standing up for yourself and asking for what you want. Likewise, if physical or emotional intimacy brings up feelings of anxiety, insecurity, or vulnerability, then you may avoid being intimate.

Thinking strategies. You may try many different ways to think your way out of your pain: trying to figure out why you feel this way, rehashing the past, beating yourself up, blaming your partner, telling yourself *I shouldn't be feeling this way*, analyzing your partner, debating with yourself, using positive affirmations, fantasizing about leaving, challenging negative thoughts and replacing them with positive ones, telling yourself to *get a grip* or *suck it up*, and so on.

Substances. You may try to push your feelings away by putting substances into your body: cigarettes, alcohol, ice cream, chocolate, pizza, nicotine, caffeine, sugar, recreational drugs, and so on.

Most STRUGGLE strategies give short-term relief from painful thoughts and feelings. But it's rarely long-lasting. Soon, those unwanted thoughts and feelings are back (sometimes even more intensely than before). You've probably also noticed that the more intense and painful your thoughts and feelings, the less effective your STRUGGLE strategies are. If you're extremely anxious, furious, or sad, or consumed by worry or hopelessness, then eating chocolate or drinking beer or browsing social media is unlikely to give you much relief, if any. STRUGGLE strategies aren't usually problematic, provided we use them flexibly and moderately. But if we use them rigidly or excessively, they quickly sap our health and well-being.

For example, if you over-rely on distraction, you waste large amounts of time doing stuff that's not fulfilling or meaningful. (Let's be honest: How many hours of your life have you wasted watching crappy television or YouTube videos? Even something as innocuous as hanging out on social media can destroy a relationship—if you do it to such a degree that you neglect to invest time and energy in your partner.)

Similarly, if you do too much opting out, you may end up cut off, isolated, and alienated from your partner, which drains all the intimacy and openness from your relationship. If you overdo it with the thinking strategies, you waste huge amounts of time inside-the-mind. And the more you rely on pumping substances into your body, the more likely you are to end up with serious health problems (including addiction).

Thus the more you STRUGGLE, the worse your quality of life suffers. And of course, we all do it at times. It only becomes an issue when we STRUGGLE *excessively*. So if the strategy you use isn't harming you or your partner, or damaging your relationship, there's no problem. But if it *is* sucking the vitality from your relationship, or affecting your health and well-being, or holding you back from making important changes, then it's wise to try a different way of responding.

What's the Alternative?

The term "hooked" technically means you're responding to your thoughts or feelings *inflexibly*: in OBEY mode, STRUGGLE mode, or both. So what's the alternative? You guessed it: *unhooking*. Unhooking means, rather than trying to avoid or get rid of difficult thoughts and feelings, we "take a step back," open up and make room for them, and allow them to freely flow through us. We give them plenty of space, so they can come, stay, and go of their own accord, without getting in our way or jerking us around. This doesn't mean we like, want, or approve of them—it simply means we *allow* them; we don't waste our precious time and energy in futile STRUGGLE.

Similarly, when you unhook, you no longer OBEY your thoughts and feelings; you are no longer mindless, reactive, on autopilot. Instead, you are aware of your thoughts and feelings, and able to consciously control your actions— so you can behave like the person you want to be. (This may not yet make sense, but it soon will.) Suffice it to say, no matter how intense your thoughts and feelings, once you unhook, they don't control you. You are no longer an automaton; you can now consciously choose what you say and do.

But hey, don't take my word for it. Over the next few chapters, you'll learn quite a few unhooking skills, so play around with them, and see for yourself what happens. Let's begin with one called...

Dropping Anchor

Ever been caught in an "emotional storm"? Distressing thoughts blowing wildly around inside your head? Painful emotions flash-flooding through your body? Emotional storms may include anger, anxiety, sadness, loneliness, guilt, shame, worries, judgments, traumatic memories, terrifying images, painful sensations, intense urges—you name it. They vary enormously in terms of composition and intensity, and no two are ever exactly the same. But there are two things they all have in common: they're painful and they easily sweep us away.

Now let's put emotional storms aside, and think about real ones. Suppose you're on a boat, and you're sailing into harbor, when your radio suddenly announces there's a storm on the way. You'd want to drop anchor quickly and securely, right? If not, your boat might get smashed or dragged out to sea. So you drop anchor, to hold the boat steady. And dropping anchor doesn't get rid of the storm. It just holds the boat steady, while the storm comes and goes in its own good time. Now what if you could do something like this with your emotional storms? Well, the good news is you can. The first step is simply to...

Notice and Name

To "notice and name" means you notice your thoughts and feelings with curiosity, and name them in a nonjudgmental manner. For example, after noticing feelings of anger or anxiety, you may silently say, "Here's anxiety" or "I'm noticing anger." This may seem like an odd thing to do, but it serves an important purpose: when we notice and name difficult thoughts and feelings, it reduces their effect on our behavior. You may find that hard to believe, but the science behind it is solid. The simple act of noticing what you are thinking or feeling, then putting it into words, activates a specific region of your brain. Situated directly behind your forehead, this region is called the "prefrontal cortex." When we "notice and name" our thoughts and feelings, the prefrontal cortex is activated, and it then moderates other parts of the brain: the ones that are fueling the emotional storm.

In other words, the less awareness we have of our thoughts and feelings, the less control we have over what we say and do. Do you recall what happened in school if your teacher left the classroom? All hell broke loose, right? Well, the same principle applies to the world inside us. Our awareness is like the teacher; our thoughts and our feelings are like the children. If we're not consciously aware of them, they "run riot." Said differently: the less our ability to notice and name our difficult thoughts and feelings, the more control they have over our behavior.

And what happens when the teacher returns to the classroom? The children immediately settle down. Similarly, when we notice and name our thoughts and feelings, they lose their power and impact. They're still present, of course; noticing and naming doesn't get rid of them. But we no longer respond in OBEY mode or STRUGGLE mode.

Here are two useful phrases for noticing and naming: "I'm noticing" and "Here is." For example, you might silently say: "I'm noticing anger," "Here's anxiety," "I'm noticing my mind racing," "Here's a feeling of loneliness," "I'm noticing an urge to drink," "Here is a knot in my stomach," "I'm noticing the thought that my partner doesn't love me."

When we first use this unusual type of self-talk, it feels a bit odd or uncomfortable. But it's worth practicing because it usually helps us unhook, at least a little. It's obviously very different than everyday language, where we say things like, "I'm anxious." That phrase makes it sound like *I am* the feeling. But if we say, "I'm noticing anxiety," or "Here is anxiety," or "Here is *a feeling of* anxiety," we can "step back" a little and see this as an emotion passing through.

Likewise, if I say, "I'm useless," it seems as if *I am* that thought; I truly am "useless." But when I say, "I'm noticing the thought 'I'm useless,'" I get a little distance from it; I can see that thought as something passing through me, rather than the essence of who I am.

If this seems odd or confusing or you don't really get it, don't be concerned. In later chapters, we'll explore this in much more depth. You'll do some "notice and name" exercises, and see for yourself how it works. At this point, I'm simply explaining the concept, because it's a key component of dropping anchor.

The ACE Formula

Now before we start dropping anchor, an important reminder: this isn't a way to avoid or get rid of stormy thoughts and feelings; anchors do not control the weather. It's a way to hold yourself steady so the storm doesn't carry you away.

You can "drop anchor" any time, any place, in hundreds of different ways, with a simple three-step formula. (And I hope you'll play around with this formula to create your own exercises, which you can make as short or as long as you wish.)

The three-step formula is "ACE":

A: acknowledge your thoughts and feelings

C: connect with your body

E: engage in what you're doing.

We'll go through the exercise now, and I'll explain it as we go. (And if you'd like my voice to guide you through it, use the free audio in chapter 6 of "Extra Bits.") You'll get the greatest benefits from this exercise if you first dredge up some painful thoughts and feelings to work with (e.g., anxiety, sadness, guilt, anger, or loneliness). So with that aim in mind, please think of a major problem in your relationship, dwell on it for a minute or so, and see if you can tap into some of that pain. (If you can't do this, it's not a problem; you can practice dropping anchor no matter what thoughts and feelings are present—whether you're confident, relaxed, and happy or miserable, anxious, and numb. But the results are much more obvious if you're at least somewhat distressed when you do it.)

A: Acknowledge Your Thoughts and Feelings

Remember how as a kid, you were so curious about the world? You could stare with fascination at an insect, or a flower, or a bird that adults would barely notice. Your challenge now is to bring that childlike curiosity to whatever is happening within your inner world. Notice whatever is "showing up" inside you: thoughts, feelings, memories, urges, or sensations.

(Note: Some people find it easier to notice thoughts than feelings; others find the opposite. Initially notice whatever is easiest for you; later tackle the harder part. If you can only notice one or the other, that's fine for now; as you work through the book that will change.)

Take about ten to twenty seconds to notice your thoughts. Take the same time again to scan your body: observe it from head to toe, and notice what sensations are present. Use a phrase like "I'm noticing" or "Here is," to name whatever you notice. For example: "Here is a feeling of sadness," "I'm noticing thoughts about ending this relationship."

The aim is to "notice and name" your thoughts and feelings, without OBEYING them and without STRUGGLING against them. Simply acknowledge that here and now, in this moment, these thoughts and feelings are present. Please do this now, before reading on, for at least twenty to thirty seconds. (That's the bare minimum; you can take much longer if you prefer.)

C: Connect with Your Body

Continue to acknowledge your thoughts and feelings, while simultaneously connecting with some part of your body. Ideally, move or stretch that body part, to help you tune into it. Following are some suggestions; please modify them as you wish, or create your own alternatives, to better suit your needs:

- Slowly and gently push your feet into the floor.

- Slowly and gently straighten up your back and your spine.

- Slowly and gently press your hands together, touching only at the fingertips.

- Slowly and gently stretch out your arms, then stretch your neck or roll your shoulders.

If there are limits to what you can do with your body because of illness, injury, or chronic pain—or if there are parts of your body you don't want to focus on—then modify the exercise accordingly. You may prefer to:

- Slowly and gently breathe in and out.

- In ultra-slow motion, ever so gently, adjust your position in your chair (or bed) to one that's more comfortable, while carefully noticing which muscles you use to do so.

- Slowly and gently raise your eyebrows as high as you can, then ever so slowly, lower them.

Use your creativity; anything you can do that helps you tune into some part of your body, from tapping your fingers to wiggling your toes, is good. You could:

- Push your palms hard against each other and feel the muscles contract in your neck, arms, and shoulders.

- Press your hands down on the arms of your chair or firmly massage the back of your neck and scalp.

- Slowly look around the room and notice how you're using your neck, head, and eyes.

- Slowly stretch.

- Twiddle your thumbs, cup your hands, give yourself a hug, slide your hands over your knees…or hundreds of other possibilities.

And if you're around other people but don't want them to know you're doing this, simply straighten up your spine and push your feet into the floor.

Remember, you're not trying to get rid of these difficult thoughts and feelings. (Anchors don't make storms go away.) Nor are you trying to distract yourself from them. (Distraction is a form of STRUGGLE.)

The aim is to keep acknowledging your thoughts and feelings, and at the same time, tune into and actively move some part(s) of your body. This is to give you more control of your physical actions, so you can act more effectively, even as the emotional storm rages.

Please do this now, before reading on: acknowledge your thoughts and feelings and connect with your body, for at least ten to twenty seconds (or longer if you wish).

E: Engage in What You're Doing

Continue to acknowledge your thoughts and feelings, and connect with your body, and as you're doing so, get a sense of where you are and what's going on. Take a moment to notice the world around you, with all your senses: notice what you can see and hear and touch and taste and smell, then focus your attention on whatever activity you are doing.

Again, please be creative and find your own methods for doing this. Here are some ideas:

- Look around the room and notice five things you can see.

- Notice three or four things you can hear.

- Notice what you can smell, taste, or sense inside your nose or mouth.

- Notice what you are doing.

Please do this now, taking ten to twenty seconds (bare minimum) to notice the world around you, then bring your full attention back to your current activity: reading this book.

✷ ✷ ✷

Well done. Now please run through the ACE steps again: *acknowledge* your thoughts and feelings; *connect* with your body; *engage* in what you're doing. Take at least ten seconds for each step (but more if preferred).

✷ ✷ ✷

You're doing really well. Now run through ACE a third time. Take at least ten seconds (or more) for each step.

✷ ✷ ✷

And now, a fourth and final time, using at least ten seconds for each step. Finish the exercise by giving your full attention to the activity you're doing (in this case, reading a book).

✷ ✷ ✷

So what happened for you? Hopefully you experienced at least one or more of the following:

- Although your thoughts and feelings probably didn't change much, you were able to separate a little from them: to "step back" and notice them, instead of getting swept away by them. You were less pushed around, bothered, or impacted by them.

- You were able to feel and move your body more readily; you had a greater sense of control over your physical actions.

- You were more present, awake, or alert.

- You had a greater awareness of where you are, what you're doing, and what you're thinking and feeling.

- You had a sense of disentangling yourself from your thoughts.

If none of that happened, or if you had problems, please see the trouble-shooting guide in "Extra Bits."

It's Not Working!

When I first take them through dropping anchor, some people say, "It isn't working!"

So I ask, "What do you mean by 'not working'?"

They usually reply, "I don't feel any better. It's not making these feelings go away."

"Yes, that's not the aim of it," I say. "We're not trying to get rid of these thoughts and feelings; anchors don't make storms go away."

If you're hurting badly, your pain is unlikely to go away as you drop anchor. However, its power will often drain away, so it can't so easily push you around. And if you keep going for several minutes—usually three or four is enough, but sometimes longer is needed—you'll often experience a sense of calmness, even when the storm continues to rage.

On the other hand, if your pain isn't that intense—for example, if you're experiencing mild frustration, sadness, or anxiety—then as you drop anchor the pain will often quickly lessen, and sometimes even completely disappear. So by all means, enjoy that when it happens, but remember: *that's not the aim.* And if that comment seems odd, it's hardly surprising. For most of us, this radically new way of responding to our difficult thoughts and feelings takes quite a while to sink in. But it's important to understand the point of dropping anchor, because otherwise, you might turn it into another STRUGGLE strategy, which is a recipe for failure and disappointment. The aims of it are:

- To gain more control over our physical actions so we can act more effectively when difficult thoughts and feelings are present

- To reduce the influence of our thoughts and feelings so they can't jerk us around (as in OBEY mode); when we're consciously aware of them—acknowledging them with curiosity—they lose much of their impact on our behavior

- To interrupt worrying, rumination, obsessing, or any other way we get lost inside-the-mind

- To interrupt our away moves (i.e., to short-circuit problematic behaviors that take us away from the life we want to build)

- To help focus (and refocus) our attention on the task or activity we are doing—especially if we're disengaged, on automatic pilot, or getting pulled out of it by our thoughts and feelings (this is why the exercise ends with the instruction to focus on what you're doing)

There are other benefits, too, which we'll cover later, but first I need to highlight that…

Distraction Is Not the Aim

The word "distraction" comes from the Latin *distrahere*, which means "draw away from." Distraction techniques are STRUGGLE strategies. The aim of them is to take your attention away from unwanted thoughts and feelings. But dropping anchor is the very opposite of distraction; instead, we actively notice whatever thoughts and feelings are present. If we try to distract ourselves—to turn away from these difficult inner experiences, ignore them, pretend they aren't there—this is yet another form of STRUGGLE.

That doesn't mean that distraction is "wrong" or "bad." It's not. A little bit of distraction, used here and there appropriately, is rarely a problem and sometimes very helpful. But hey, you already know how to distract yourself; you've got a zillion and one different ways to do it. And you also know they often don't work, or if they do, it's usually just short-term relief. So our aim here is to do something radically different: to "drop the struggle" with difficult thoughts and feelings; let them be; open up and make room for them; allow them to freely come, stay, and go in their own good time.

Mixing It Up

There are hundreds of ways to use the ACE formula, so please play around with it and create your own techniques for dropping anchor. Also, consider altering the sequence; it needn't be:

Acknowledge → *Connect* → *Engage*.

Some people prefer:

Connect → *Acknowledge* → *Engage*.

Or:

Engage → *Connect* → *Acknowledge*.

The sequence doesn't matter as long as you include all three phases and you run through several cycles. (Remember, don't skip the *acknowledge* phase, or it will become distraction.) You can also experiment with simpler methods of naming; for example, some people like to use just one word: "Anger," "Worrying," "Loneliness," "Judging."

Now, please drop anchor again, and do at least three cycles of ACE.

So What's Next?

After you drop anchor, what's next? Well, if the activity you're doing is a toward move (taking you toward the life you want to build and the person you want to be), then keep doing it. And as you do it, give it your full attention. Why? For two good reasons.

One: if we want to do anything well, we need to keep our attention on what we're doing. It doesn't matter how skilled, knowledgeable, experienced, or talented we may be; if we can't stay focused on the task, we won't do it well. This is what elite athletes mean when after a poor performance they say, "My head wasn't in the game." But this doesn't just apply to athletes. It applies to all of us, whatever we are doing: riding a bike, washing dishes, making love, writing an email, supervising the kids, reading a book, or working at our job. If we're disengaged, unfocused, distracted, or simply "going through the motions," then we will not do these things well.

Two: when we give our full attention to the activity we're doing, we'll find it more rewarding and fulfilling. Basically, the less attention we give to what we're doing, the less satisfaction or pleasure we'll get from doing it (for reasons we'll explore later).

So if, after dropping anchor, you're doing a toward move, give your full attention to that activity. But if you're doing an away move, then stop and do a toward move instead.

When and Where?

The more we practice dropping anchor, the better. So run through the steps of ACE repeatedly throughout the day whenever you're mild to moderately stressed, anxious, angry, irritable, worried, or sad. Then as your skills improve, test them out in harsher weather conditions. It may take a while, but with continued practice you'll find you can drop anchor in even the roughest of storms. (But you do have to practice. If you read a book about how to play tennis, that won't make you a good player; you have to go out on the court and practice your shots.)

It's also helpful to drop anchor whenever you're unfocused, distracted, or on automatic pilot; it will help you refocus and engage. Similarly, when you're feeling sluggish, drained, lethargic, or like you "can't be bothered doing anything," this can help you wake up, energize, and regain control of your actions. (However, keep in mind: you need to adapt everything in this book to suit your own unique life situation. So if your lethargy is due to sleep deprivation or a medical condition, it may, at times, be better to go and lie down rather than wake yourself up through dropping anchor.)

The great thing about these exercises is that they are so incredibly easy to fit into your daily routine; you can do them anytime, anywhere, as often as desired: a thirty-second version while you're stopped at a red light; or a one-minute version when you first get out of bed; a two-minute version while waiting in a slow-moving line; or a five-minute version during your lunch break. You can even do it lying in bed—assuming you want to wake up and get out of it. (If you're wanting to drift off to sleep, don't drop anchor; it's designed to increase your alertness, not lower it!)

It's particularly useful to drop anchor:

- When any type of emotional storm blows up

- When you keep going inside-the-mind: worrying, obsessing, fantasizing, ruminating, etc.

- When you want to interrupt any type of self-defeating behavior

- When it's hard to focus on or engage in what you're doing

- When you want to switch off OBEY mode or STRUGGLE mode (or both)

As with any new skill, the more you practice, the better the results. Ten minutes a day is great, and twenty is even better. But even *just one minute* is better than nothing. And please be patient; you may not notice much benefit at first. On the other hand, you may quickly notice a dramatic difference. Most likely, you'll be somewhere between those extremes. But if you practice this regularly and often, even for just a few minutes a day, it will, over time, pay big dividends.

CHAPTER 7

Into the Smog

Suppose a miracle happened and your partner suddenly became your perfect "soul mate": no faults at all, no annoying habits, always there for you, able to meet your every need and desire.

- If that happened, how would *you* change?

- What would you stop or start doing; what would you do more of and less of?

- What personal qualities would you work on?

- What attitude would you cultivate toward your partner?

- How would you respond to them when they're hurting? How would you treat them when they fail, make mistakes, or screw up?

Please consider or write about this for a few minutes.

✷ ✷ ✷

So what did you learn about yourself? Did you discover a gap between the way you'd *ideally* behave (if magic happened) and the way you *actually* behave, in the real world? If yes, that means you're normal; the more stressful and challenging your relationship, the larger this gap tends to be. However, with time, effort, and practice you can bridge that gap, and the first step is simply to acknowledge it's there.

At this point, notice what your mind is telling you. Often our mind tries hard to justify the gap: "I wouldn't be acting this way if he would just do X, Y, and Z" or "If she would just stop *that*, I wouldn't do *this*." Although such thoughts are normal, they are not helpful. They easily pull us into our own...

Psychological Smog

The mind is a masterful storyteller. All day long, it tells us story after story, repeatedly captivating our attention. In everyday language, we call these stories "thoughts," or more technically "cognitions." In ACT, we prefer to call them "stories," because that term often helps reduce their impact. But sometimes people protest: "It's not a story! It's true!" So I explain that "story" does not mean something false, exaggerated, or made up. It simply means a string of words that convey information.

A story *may* be objectively true, in which case we call it a "fact." But most of our mind's stories are not "facts"; mostly they are opinions, judgments, beliefs, attitudes, ideas, assumptions, rules, expectations, dreams, fears, fantasies, and so on. (If you don't like the term "story," then each time you see it in this book, please convert it in your head to "thought" or "cognition.")

Our mind has an endless supply of stories, and while some of them are pleasant, enjoyable, and helpful, many of them are the opposite: unhelpful, difficult, or painful. And when such stories hook us, they create a thick black cloud of "psychological smog." And just like real smog, it surrounds us, smothers us, and prevents us from seeing clearly or acting effectively. Usually, several types of stories intermingle and coalesce to produce psychological smog. Read through the following list of common types and consider which ones your mind likes to tell:

"Should" Stories

"Should" stories have themes like:

- Why *should* I bother?

- It's not my problem; I *shouldn't* have to change.

- They *should* change first!

- Why *should* I make it easy for them?

- They *shouldn't* have treated me that way.

- They *should* apologize and admit they're wrong.

- It *shouldn't* be this hard.

When we get hooked by these thoughts, we become righteous, indignant, angry, or resentful. The word "should" (along with similar words like "must," "ought," and "have to") implies there is a rule that must be obeyed. And if our partner doesn't follow that rule, we get upset. Take a moment to consider: What does your mind say your partner *should* do?

According to your mind, *should* your partner: Know what you want? Respect your wishes? Put their clothes away? Approve of your friends? Spend more time on foreplay? Have more interest in sex?

The human mind is like a "should factory": it churns out those "shoulds," "musts," and "oughts" in a never-ending stream, in all sorts of shapes and sizes. You may insist, "But it's true; they *should* put their clothes away." Well, that may indeed be true (there are many, many people who'd agree with you)—but is it *helpful?* What happens to your relationship when you get hooked by "shoulds"? Doesn't it just ramp up your resentment, disappointment, or dissatisfaction? Doesn't it just increase the tension and conflict?

"No Point Trying" Stories

These stories tell us that the future is all doom and gloom, so there's no point trying. For example:

- It's too late. There's too much damage. We can never repair it, so why waste my time?

- She'll never change, so why should I make the effort?

Most of us have thoughts like this at times, especially when the going gets tough. But what happens if you let these thoughts push you around? What happens to your relationship if you "go along with the story" and give up?

"If Only" Stories

These stories are composed of wishful thinking:

- If only he would get his act together...

- If only she would get off my back...

- If only he would share his feelings more openly...

- If only she could get on better with my parents...

We all get absorbed in wishful thinking at times. It's a temporary escape into fantasy. But the more time we spend in the land of "if only," the more dissatisfied we are with the land of "reality." When you get hooked by "If only," does it help you to improve your relationship in any way? Or does it just breed discontentment?

"Painful Past" Stories

These ones recount all your most painful memories, when your partner screwed up, or hurt you, or let you down. We don't have to try hard to recall them; as soon as things get tense, our mind starts streaming its own personal YouTube channel, in maximum resolution, with the sound cranked up to full volume. And we readily watch them, end to end, even though nothing useful ever comes of it. Consider: Has dwelling on painful memories ever been useful for your relationship? Or does it just foster hurt, resentment, anxiety, guilt, or anger?

"Scary Future" Stories

These are frightening predictions about the future. Often they warn us not to change our behavior, because if we do:

- My partner will take advantage of me.

- I'll get hurt.

- They won't take responsibility.

- They'll never change.

- They'll just do it again.

- They'll take me for granted.

- I'll be stuck in this relationship, and it'll just get worse.

- I'm making the wrong choice; I'd be happier with someone else.

We all imagine scary future scenarios. That's normal. It's our mind doing a very important job: anticipating threats and dangers in order to protect and keep us safe. Indeed, a normal human mind is constantly on the lookout for anything that might harm or hurt us—now or in the future. It's an essential mental ability, and if our mind *doesn't* do this, then we're in trouble. Unfortunately, though, this useful mental skill often mutates into "worrying," "stressing out," or "obsessing."

Please consider:

- What are the scariest stories your mind likes to tell you?

- When you get hooked by these stories, what tends to happen? Does it help you take action to improve your relationship? Does it help you grow closer to your partner?

- When these stories hook you, does that hold you back from making important changes? Or bolster your urge to give up or run away?

"Why I Can't or Won't" Stories

These stories consist of all our reasons for why we can't or won't or shouldn't change:

- I'm too depressed/stressed/tired/run-down.

- I've had enough. I've got no energy left to try anymore.

- I'm happy with who I am. She needs to change, not me.

- I'm too old to change.

- I've always been this way. This is the way I am. Take it or leave it.

- I just don't care anymore.

- If he changes first, then I'll change!

Our minds are brilliant at reason-giving. And in the short run, if we go along with these reasons not to change, it's quite convenient: it helps us avoid all the discomfort of facing our fears, tackling our problems, changing our behavior. But what happens in the long run? If you get hooked by these reasons not to change—and allow them to dictate what you do—what is the long-term effect upon your relationship?

"Bad Partner" Stories

These consist of all the negative judgments our mind makes about our partner:

- She's a bitch.

- He's a loser.

- He's too much X.

- She's not Y enough.

- They don't deserve to be treated well!

- They're driving me crazy!

- They're the one with the issues, not me!

Consider: What sort of judgments does your mind make about your partner?

- When your mind really wants to do a "hatchet job"—to cut your partner into little pieces—what are the harshest judgments or nastiest names it comes up with?

- What happens to your relationship when you get hooked by these judgments? How do you feel when you get all caught up in them?

- If you let these thoughts dictate what you say and do, what happens to your relationship?

"I'm Not Good Enough" Stories

These ones consist of all our harsh self-judgments. *I'm…fat, stupid, ugly, broken, worthless, lazy, boring, unlovable, weird, a loser…*and so on. When you get hooked by "I'm not good enough," how do you feel? And what do you tend to say and do? And does that help or hinder your relationship?

"Superior/Inferior" Stories

Variants on "Bad Partner" and "I'm Not Good Enough," these stories emphasize comparisons to our partner. Our mind may insist that we are superior, smarter, or stronger than our partner. Or it may state the opposite: we are inferior, dumber, or weaker than our partner.

When hooked by "I'm superior," we may look down on our partner, dismiss their ideas, discount their needs, ignore their rights, or lack consideration for them in other ways. When hooked by "I'm inferior," we may become insecure, anxious, fearful of rejection, needy for reassurance, demanding of approval, or neglectful of our own needs and rights. So holding on tightly to either of these stories—"superior" or "inferior"—is not useful.

Your mind may not go along with this idea. It may protest, *But it's true!* And let's face it, if your mind wants to "prove" you're "superior," it *can* find ways in which you surpass your partner. And if your mind wants to "prove" you're "inferior," it *can* find ways your partner surpasses you. This is always possible, because any two humans will have different "strengths" and "weaknesses." (I've put "strengths" and "weaknesses" in quotes because these are *judgments*, not *facts*. What one person judges a weakness, another may see as a strength. For example, I judge it a strength that I am able to cry freely when I am sad; yet some people might judge this a weakness, especially if hooked by the rule that "Men don't cry!")

If your mind wants to make you feel superior, it just needs to focus on the ways in which you are "stronger." Or if it wants you to feel inferior, it can highlight the ways you are "weaker." If you look hard enough, there will be no shortage of either. So rather than debate whether your self-judgment is "true or false," consider: Is it helpful? When it hooks you, what do you typically say and do? And does that help you build the relationship you want?

When hooked by "I'm superior," we *do* feel better about ourself, *but* it breeds arrogance, selfishness, and narcissism and, worse, a lack of consideration for our partner—for their ideas, opinions, feelings, rights, and needs. Conversely, when we're hooked by "I'm inferior," we may experience insecurity, jealousy, depression, anxiety, or neediness; neglect important values like self-care, self-protection, and self-respect; and dismiss or neglect our own rights and needs.

"I Know Why" Stories

In these stories, your mind analyzes your partner and tries to figure out why they keep thinking, feeling, or doing those things you find difficult: *Why can't they just stop?! Why do they keep doing that?!* Your mind comes up with all sorts of plausible ideas: unconscious motivations, hidden desires, secret agendas, fundamental flaws. Minds can be endlessly inventive with this stuff. Consider: How does your mind explain your partner's behavior? Does it ever say things like:

- She's doing it on purpose, to prove a point.

- He's doing it to hurt me.

- She could change if she really wanted to. She just can't be bothered.

- He's got an unconscious hostility toward women.

- It's because deep down inside she wants to leave me.

Analyzing your partner is a fascinating game, and the results can seem very convincing. But what happens when you treat those assumptions as facts, give them all your attention, dwell on them, or let them guide your actions? Does that help you build a better relationship?

"Blame" Stories

Blending seamlessly into "Bad Partner" stories and "Shoulds," these ones are full of accusation and judgment:

- They're to blame!

- It's their fault!

- If they hadn't done that, this would never have happened.

- Why do they keep doing that? If they'd just stop, there wouldn't be any problem!

- They shouldn't have done that. They had no right.

These stories may also include self-blame. We accuse ourselves, find ourselves guilty, and pass judgment: *It's all my fault! I'm to blame!* (And this, of course, feeds "I'm not good enough.")

"Deep-Seated Fear" Stories

Deep-seated fears can often get in the way of our values. Common ones include:

- Fear of being abandoned or rejected

- Fear of being smothered or controlled

- Fear of being ignored, taken for granted, or neglected

- Fear of being hurt or harmed

- Fear of being manipulated, deceived, or betrayed

Often these deep-seated fears go right back to childhood. Remember that brief account of attachment theory in chapter 4? If as a child one (or more) of your caregivers was aggressive, neglectful, or unreliable, naturally you'll have deep-seated fears about similar things recurring in other relationships. These fears may surface as utterly compelling stories, such as:

- He's going to leave me. I couldn't bear to be without him.

- I'm not good enough for her. I know she'll find someone better.

- He's trying to control me. He won't let me be who I am.

- If I give her what she wants, there'll be nothing left of me.

- When he finds out what I'm really like, he'll leave.

When deep-seated fears hook you, what happens to your behavior? If you let those fears guide what you say and do, does that help you bond with your partner, or does it increase the distance between you?

Your Mind Is Like an Overly Helpful Friend

Do you recognize any of the thoughts listed previously? If so, you're normal. We all have at least some layers of this smog showing up at times. (Personally, at various times, I experience *all* of them!) We can't stop unhelpful thoughts from arising. I'm assuming you've already discovered this for yourself. But if not, don't take my word: check it out. Try to stop your mind from generating unhelpful thoughts. Try to think nothing but helpful thoughts—and see how long you last before an unhelpful one appears. Or try to push those thoughts out of your head—and notice just how quickly they come bouncing back. Or try to challenge them—and notice how much time and effort that requires, having a full-on debate with your own mind. (And even if you win that debate temporarily, notice how quickly those very same thoughts reappear; they won't remain "defeated" for long.)

Of course, you may find that these thoughts give you a break at times—when you're in a great mood, or you're on vacation, or your partner is on their best behavior—but you've undoubtedly discovered that as soon as your mood takes a downturn, or your stress levels increase, or your partner's behavior lapses, those thoughts immediately spring back into action. And some of those thoughts are very old, aren't they? Some of them have been around since the early days of your relationship. And many of them have been present in other previous relationships. (I'm no mind reader; it's like this for all of us. Smoggy thoughts are rarely brand-new. Usually they're variants of old stories that have been showing up for years in other relationships.)

So why does a normal human mind naturally generate so many unhelpful thoughts? I'm glad you asked. Have you ever had an overly helpful friend, who was trying sooooo hard to help you, they actually became a nuisance? Although they had good intentions, they kept getting in the way or annoying you, making things harder? Well, that's what's going on when your mind generates all these smoggy stories. Your mind's not out to sabotage, punish, or hurt you; it's not deliberately trying to make your life harder. On the contrary, your mind is continually trying to help you get what you want, or avoid what you don't want, or both. And almost every thought it generates is *intended* to serve one or both of those purposes.

For an obvious example, consider all your worries, anxieties, "deep-seated fears," and "scary futures"; this is your mind trying to help keep you safe and prevent you from getting hurt. It's warning you about things that may hurt or harm you, so you can "prepare for the worst," so that if something bad does actually happen, you can act effectively. The "No Point Trying" stories also serve the same basic purpose: your mind's telling you these things because it's trying to save you from the enormous pain you'll have if you work hard but ultimately fail.

What about all those "Painful Past" stories? Well, that's your mind trying to help you learn from your past experiences and mistakes, so that if something similar ever happens in the future, you'll be better prepared. "I Know Why" and "If Only" stories serve the same purpose. By getting you to figure out why things happened as they did, or imagine how things might have worked out better, your mind is trying to help you learn from the past and prepare for the future. That way, if similar events ever happen again, you'll know how to handle them better.

Then there are all those judgments—about yourself, your partner, or both. Judgments are your mind's attempt to help you rapidly make sense of what's going on. "This is good, positive, safe," "That's bad, negative, dangerous," "He's ugly," "She's beautiful," "I'm fat," "You're slim," "You can't trust those people," "This relationship sucks," "I'm right, you're wrong!" and so on. That judgment factory in our head churns out its product all day long. Why? Because our mind's trying hard to map out our world, quickly and simply: to point out what's "safe" and "good" and highlight what's "unsafe" and "bad." This saves us expending a lot of mental effort carefully considering whether things are good or bad.

So when your mind judges your partner, it's basically saying: "Watch out! You need to do something about that!" Again, your mind is preparing you by pointing out problems, in the hope you'll do something about them. "Blaming" yourself or your partner serves the same purpose: your mind's trying to help by pointing out who's at fault and what they did, in the hope you'll learn from this experience and prepare yourself better for next time.

And when your mind judges *you*, it's basically trying to "whip you into shape." It wants to help you change your behavior: to stop doing things that might get you hurt and start doing things to make your life better. The mind figures if it leans on you hard enough, beats you up enough, then you'll "sort yourself out," "shape up," or "do the right thing."

And let's not forget the "shoulds." Your mind loves to lay down strict rules about what you can, can't, should, or shouldn't do: "Can't do this!" and "Have to do that!" This is your mind giving you guidelines for life: do this, and you'll be okay; do that, and you'll be in trouble. The intention, yet again, is to help you get what you want and avoid what you don't want. Your mind also assumes that your partner *should* obey your rules—because that will make your life better—and it gets angry when your partner doesn't do as expected. The message: *make them follow your rules and you'll be okay; if they don't comply, expect trouble!*

Now as I said earlier, some smoggy thoughts may be true. But in ACT, we are rarely concerned about whether our thoughts (or cognitions) are true or false. Our main interest is: Are these thoughts *helpful*? If these thoughts guide what we say and do, will we behave like the person we want to be and build the sort of life we want to live? Will these thoughts help us choose toward moves? Will they help us do things that heal and strengthen our relationship—or will they guide us into actions that destroy it?

If our thoughts are helpful, it makes sense to use them, to let them guide what we say and do. But if not, it's wise to *unhook* from them. Remember:

It is *not* your thoughts themselves that create the smog.

Smog only happens *when we get hooked!*

It's so important to recognize this. Our thoughts, in and of themselves, aren't a problem. *Getting hooked by our thoughts:* that's the problem. So how do we unhook and emerge from the smog? Well, one thing we don't do is STRUGGLE. We don't challenge, dispute, or fight with our thoughts; we don't push them away, or suppress them, or try to distract ourselves; we don't try to rewrite them as "positive thoughts." Instead, we emerge from the smog through a simple three-step process called...

CHAPTER 8

Notice, Name, Refocus

Are you ready to emerge from the smog? We can't stop smoggy thoughts from arising. They're normal and natural, and our mind (being an "overly helpful friend") will keep on cranking them out. But we can learn to unhook from them, to step out of the smog and get on with our life. In this chapter, we're going to focus on judgments because they are the most common smoggy thoughts. However, the methods we cover can be used with any type of cognition. Let's kick off with a look at harsh self-judgment.

EXERCISE: Notice and Name Your Self-Judgments

What does your mind say when it really wants to beat you up? When it turns into judge, jury, and executioner and lays out all the evidence about what's wrong with you? If I could listen in to your mind, what would I hear it saying?

Pull out your journal, or use the worksheet in "Extra Bits" and jot down some of the things your mind says. Complete each sentence with as many words or phrases as you can think of.

When it wants to judge me as "not good enough"...

- My mind tells me that I am a...

- My mind tells me that I am too...

- My mind tells me that I am not enough of a...

- My mind tells me that I do too much of the following:

- My mind tells me that I don't do enough of the following:

- My mind tells me that I lack the following:

* * *

Once you've done that, read through the list, pick the self-judgment that bothers you most, and shorten it to between two and six words—for example, I'm boring, I'm too selfish, or I'm not smart enough.

* * *

Done that? Good. Next, we'll do some work with "noticing and naming," building on the methods introduced in chapter 5. But first, you need to let that judgment hook you; buy into it, give it all your attention, believe it as much as possible. This may make you feel a bit yucky, but it's important; you can't practice *unhooking* unless you are at least a little bit hooked. So, ready to give it a go?

Bring to mind your negative self-judgment—in the shortened form of "I am X"—and buy into it as much as you possibly can for ten seconds. Notice what happens.

* * *

Now silently replay that judgment in your head, but this time put a short phrase in front of it: "I'm having the thought that…" Notice what happens.

* * *

Now do that again, but the added phrase is now slightly different: "I notice I'm having the thought that…" Notice what happens.

So what happened? When you use the phrases "I'm having the thought that…" and "I notice I'm having the thought that…," most people get a sense of separation from their thought. It doesn't go away, but it loses some of its impact. In other words, you *unhooked*. (Technically, this process is called "cognitive defusion.")

I hope you unhooked at least a little with that exercise. If not, please try again with a different judgment. If yes, *also* try again with a different judgment, so you can build the skill. Ideally, try this with three or four self-judgments. Pleased do this now, before reading on.

***

When we are hooked:

- Our thoughts seem very important, as if we need to give them all our attention.

- Our thoughts seem like wise advice we should follow.

- Our thoughts seem like commands we must obey, or rules we have to follow.

- Our thoughts seem like objective facts: "the truth."

When we unhook, we separate from our thoughts and see their true nature. We realize:

- Our thoughts are basically sounds, words, pictures, or "bits of language."

- Our thoughts are not orders or rules we have to obey; we don't have to do what they tell us to do.

- Our thoughts may or may not be important; we give them our full attention only if and when it's helpful to do so.

- Our thoughts may or may not be wise; we don't automatically follow their advice.

- Our thoughts may or may not be true; we don't automatically believe them.

Unhooking helps us "take a step back" from the mind: to notice the story it's telling us without getting pulled into it; to observe how we're thinking and choose our response. When our thoughts contain useful information, we can use them for guidance. But if they're not helpful, we "let them be": we acknowledge they're present and allow them to freely come, stay, and go in their own good time.

Exercise: Watching Your Thoughts

This exercise will help you step back and watch your mind in action: to observe your thoughts coming and staying and going. (And if you want my voice to guide you, use the free audio in chapter 8 of "Extra Bits.") Please stop reading for sixty seconds, close your eyes, and notice what your mind is saying. (If your mind goes silent, wait a bit longer; eventually it will say something, even if it's just, "I'm not having any thoughts!")

* * *

Now do that again, and this time see if you can notice the *form* of your thoughts: Are they pictures, words, sounds, or objects? Do you "see" them, "hear" them, or "sense" them?

* * *

Now do that one more time, but notice where your thoughts seem to be located. Do they seem to be in front of you, behind you, above you, to one side of you, inside your head, or inside your body? Are they moving or still? If still, where are they stationed? If moving, at what speed and in which direction?

Hopefully the previous exercises helped you separate from your thoughts: to step back and observe them. The next exercise explains how this can help your relationship.

Exercise: Hands as Thoughts

Rest this book on your lap or a table, so both your hands are free. Now imagine that your hands are your thoughts. Place your hands side by side, palms upward, as if they are the pages of an open book. Hold them out in front of you. Notice that you can see your hands clearly, and you can also clearly see the room around you.

Now, once you have finished reading this sentence, ever so slooooowly raise your hands up toward your face...until they touch your face and cover your eyes. Then notice what has happened to your view of the room around you.

So what did you notice? With your hands over your eyes, you could only see bits and pieces of the room, between the slight gaps in your fingers; most of the room disappeared from view. This is what happens when hooked by our thoughts: we're so caught up in them, we lose touch with the big picture.

Now suppose your hands represent all the harsh judgments you make about your partner. And suppose your partner is standing right in front of you. What happens to your view of your partner as you bring your hands up in front of your face? That's right: the closer your hands get to your face, the less clearly you can see your partner.

Something similar happens when we're hooked by judgments. We get so entangled in our stories, we no longer see our partner as they are. All we see are the labels our mind has slapped on them: loser, selfish, lazy, uncaring, slob, bitch, demanding, needy, and so on. We lose touch with the whole human being in front of us—a person with many different facets of personality, and a wide range of strengths and weaknesses. Instead we see our partner through a filter of criticism and condemnation, and then—surprise, surprise—we end up dissatisfied and discontented.

"Yes, that's all very well," I hear you say, "but what if those judgments are true?" Good point. Remember, in ACT, we're rarely concerned about whether your thoughts are "true" or "false." We're far more interested in whether your thoughts are "helpful." In other words, if you give these thoughts all your attention, or allow them to dictate what you say and do, does that help you be the person you want to be, do the things you want to do, build the sort of relationship you want?

Now quickly do this little exercise again—and this time, notice that while your hands are covering your face, it is difficult to act effectively.

Imagine trying to drive a car or cook dinner or type on a computer like this! Similarly it's hard for you to act effectively, guided by your values, when you're blinkered by all those judgments about your partner. But if you can unhook from those judgments and tune into your values, you will notice a massive difference.

For example, suppose you want your partner to help with the housework. Your mind instantly starts telling you the "bad partner" story: *They're so lazy and selfish. Why don't they ever do any housework? I shouldn't have to ask! They take me for granted!* And if that story hooks you, what happens next? Do you snap at your partner, say something judgmental? Or perhaps you try asking them "nicely," but find it comes out laden with anger or bitterness? Or maybe you say nothing; you knuckle down and do it yourself, seething with resentment.

What if you could unhook from that story: step out of the smog, connect with your values, and behave like the partner you really want to be? You might then choose to remind yourself that your partner is different from you, so naturally they have different attitudes and habits. You might also remind yourself that your partner is your friend, not your foe, and then consider how you like to talk to your friends. Or you might choose to apply the communication, assertiveness, and negotiation skills that you'll learn in chapters 14, 15, and 16, respectively, so you can get your partner's help in a way that's both caring and considerate, as well as being healthy for the relationship. (Of course, snapping and criticizing may prompt your partner to help, but it has big costs: it makes your partner feel bad and increases the tension in your relationship.)

Calling a Spade "a Spade"

There are many different ways to unhook from judgments. One way is to notice and name them as they arise. You could silently say to yourself, *Aha! Judgment time again.* or, *Aha! Here's the "bad partner" story. I know this one.* You might also like to give your "bad partner" story a specific name—for example, The Lazy Slob Story or The Workaholic Story. Then each time you notice a thought, feeling, or memory connected to that story, you can name it: *Aha! The Workaholic Story. There it is again. I know this one.*

Unhooking from the "bad partner" story doesn't come naturally, because we're so accustomed to going along with it—but with practice, it does get easier.

Lighthearted phrases are often helpful: "Judgment Day—again!" "Aha! The judgment machine's on red alert today." Or you might simply say, "Here's judging." Over the next few weeks, play around with these methods. Try to catch the judgment machine in action, and label what it is doing; then notice what happens as a result. *Remember*: The aim is not to stop or get rid of the judgments; there's no way to stop your mind producing them. The aim is to see them for what they are: a bunch of words churned out by your mind, in its misguided attempts to help you.

Let's now try another, similar exercise—but this time, looking at judgments about your partner.

EXERCISE: Notice and Name Judgments About Your Partner

Please complete each sentence with as many words or phrases as possible.

When my mind wants to hook me with the "bad partner" story...

- It tells me that my partner is a...

- It tells me that my partner is too...

- It tells me that my partner is not enough of a...

- It tells me that my partner does too much of the following:

- It tells me that my partner doesn't do enough of the following:

- It tells me that my partner lacks the following:

* * *

Now read through the list and pick the judgment that bothers you the most and shorten it: "My partner is X" or "My partner is not Y enough."

* * *

Now hold and buy into that judgment as much as you possibly can for twenty seconds. Notice what happens.

* * *

Now silently replay that judgment in your head, but this time put a phrase in front of it: "I'm having the thought that..." Notice what happens.

* * *

Now do that again, but the added phrase is longer: "I notice I'm having the thought that..." Notice what happens.

How did you do? I hope you unhooked a little. If not, please try again with a different judgment. If yes, *also* try again with a different judgment, to build the skill. Ideally, try this with three or four judgments.

EXERCISE: Carrying Your Judgments

For this unhooking exercise, find a loose sheet of paper, blank on both sides. On one side of the sheet, write down four or five of the harshest judgments your mind makes about your partner.

* * *

Once you've done that, turn the sheet over and write in large bold capitals: AHA! THE "BAD PARTNER" STORY! HERE IT IS AGAIN! I KNOW THIS ONE!

(Change the name of the story if you think of a better one.)

* * *

Now turn the sheet back over, and slowly read through that list of all your judgments. Once you've finished, flip it over again, and read the bold capitals on the back. Notice what happens.

* * *

By now you should be somewhat unhooked. The thoughts are there, but they're having less impact. If this isn't happening, please drop anchor and run through the ACE formula (as many times as necessary) until you unhook.

So how did you fare? Most people find that method instantly helps them to unhook. (If it didn't help, or, as occasionally happens, you got even more hooked than before, then this isn't a suitable method for you—so skip it.) When this method works well for my clients, I ask them, "Would you be willing to fold that piece of paper up? And for the next week, carry it around with you in your purse or wallet? And pull it out four or five times a day? And each time you do so, first read through all the judgments, then flip it over and read what you've written on the back?" I encourage you to try this yourself (but only if the original exercise worked). While there are no guarantees with any of the techniques in this book, most clients report a week later that they are unhooking from the "bad partner" story much more easily—in which case, I ask them to extend this practice for another month.

You can also use this method to unhook from judgments about yourself. The only differences are: a) you write *self*-judgments on one side; b) on the other side, instead of "The 'Bad Partner' Story," you write "The 'I'm Not Good Enough' Story."

What About "Refocus"?

So far, we've solely focused on "notice" and "name," but the third step in this method is "refocus." And this step is exactly what it sounds like. After noticing and naming, you instantly refocus: you notice where you are, what's going on, and what you're doing. And whatever activity you're doing, you give it your full attention. (Of course, if that activity is an away move, then you ideally switch to a different one that's a toward move.)

So, there you have it: *notice, name, refocus*. And as with dropping anchor, practice is essential. You can't learn to drive by reading a book about it; you have to get in a car and practice driving. And the same goes for all the skills in this book. So in the service of building a better relation-ship, are you willing to practice the following?

- Do the Carrying Your Judgments Exercise as described previously. (But only if it worked for you!) Carry the folded paper around in your purse or wallet, and pull it out several times a day. Slowly read through the list of judgments. Then flip it over, and read the bold capitals on the back. Finally, fold it up and put it back inside your wallet or purse. Then immediately refocus: notice where you are, what's going on, what you're doing. Focus on the activity you're doing; give it your full attention, and engage in it fully.

- Throughout the day, when you catch your mind judging, silently name it. Use a phrase like, *Here's judging,* or *Aha! The "bad partner" story,* or simply, *Judging.* Also use this method with other unhelpful thoughts or patterns of thinking: *Here's worrying,* or *Aha! There's my mind laying down rules,* or simply, *Smog!* After noticing and naming, immediately refocus: notice where you are, and what's going on, then give your full attention to what you're doing.

- At times you'll get hooked before you know it. The moment you realize it's happened, notice and name it. Use a lighthearted non-judgmental phrase: *Oops! Just got hooked!* or *D'oh! Hooked again!* Then notice and name what hooked you, and refocus.

- If you can't successfully unhook with these methods, drop anchor. Run through the ACE cycle as many times as you need; often once will be enough, but sometimes you may need to run through it two to four times.

- Freely play around with the phrases I've suggested; change them into your own words, and notice what happens.

- And remember, although we've focused on judgments, you can use these methods with any type of thought. So please use them liber-ally. Experiment and see what happens. Hopefully you'll quickly emerge from your psychological smog. But if you don't, no need for alarm; there are plenty more ways to deal with…

CHAPTER 9

Gripping Stories

Have you ever been in conversation with someone, and suddenly realized you haven't heard a word they've been saying, and you're no longer sure what they're talking about? Ever driven in your car and found that when you got to the destination, you couldn't remember the journey? Ever walked into a room to get something, but once there, you couldn't remember what it was? Ever attended a social event where you were so caught up in your thoughts, you might as well not have been there?

These are just a few common examples of what happens when we're inside-the-mind. Another good example is "worrying." As mentioned earlier, to have scary thoughts is normal and natural, and need not be a problem. "Worrying" is what happens when we get *hooked* by those thoughts: giving them all our attention, replaying them over and over. "Ruminating" and "obsessing" are similar: we go over and over old hurts or painful memories; or endlessly analyze what's wrong with ourself or our partner; or fixate on something our partner said and keep wondering, *Why did they say that?!*

Worrying, ruminating, and obsessing all involve the same basic process: getting hooked by our thoughts (pulled inside-the-mind, smothered by psychological smog). Yet another way to describe this process is "holding on tightly" to your thoughts—as opposed to "easing your grip on them" and letting them freely come, stay, and go. Sticking with this metaphor, let's look at how to...

Loosen Your Grip

Clench your hand into a fist. A tight one. Have a good look at it. Notice the shape, the contours, the white knuckles. While your hand is clenched tightly, what is it good for? Only one thing: aggression. You can use it to intimidate or deliver a blow, and that's about it. A clenched fist cannot gently stroke the face of a loved one, hold the tiny hand of a newborn baby, or softly caress the contours of your partner's body.

Now gradually release the tension in your fist. Open it up, uncurl your fingers, and let your hand relax. Now you can use your hand to write, paint, type, chop vegetables, drive a car, stroke a dog, brush your teeth, caress your partner's face, cradle your baby's head, or massage your aching temples.

When we hold on to our thoughts tightly, we become inflexible. Like a clenched fist, we are limited in what we can do. And when those thoughts are critical of our partner, we are likely to say or do something hurtful. But when we "loosen the grip" on those thoughts, "hold them lightly," we become more flexible and adaptable, and we can respond more effectively to our challenges.

How to Hold Thoughts Lightly

Following are several techniques designed to help you hold your thoughts lightly. Please treat them as experiments (because no method works for everyone). And if a method backfires (don't worry, it's not common) and you end up more hooked than before, then drop anchor. (Then give that method a miss; it's not right for you.)

EXERCISE: A Fistful of Thoughts

To get the most out of this exercise, take your time as you move through each step. Read the instructions once before beginning.

Bring to mind an unhelpful story about your partner, and condense it into one sentence.

1. For about twenty seconds, get all caught up in it—buy into it; let it hook you.

2. Now hold your hand, palm upward, in front of you. Imagine taking that story out of your head and placing it onto the open palm of your hand.

3. Now slowly clench your fist as tightly as you can, gripping that story as if your life depended on it. Hold it tightly for a few seconds.

4. Ever so sloooowly, ease off your grip. Gently open your hand and let the story rest there on your palm. Don't try to flick it away or wipe it off. Just let it sit there.

5. Allowing the story to stay there, resting on your palm, gently refocus: notice where you are, what's around you, what's going on. The story is still present; you're not trying to get rid of it or distract yourself from it. You're acknowledging its present and *simultaneously* giving most of your attention to the activity you're doing here and now.

So what happened? Hopefully you unhooked at least a little. If not, try again. But if it still doesn't work, skip it and try some alternatives:

EXERCISE: Naming the Story

Earlier, we talked about noticing and naming the "bad partner" story or the "I'm not good enough" story. We can take this method further. Imagine that you can magically take every single difficult thought, feeling, and memory connected to your relationship issues and put them all into some sort of magical book. What title would you give that book, beginning with "The" and ending with "Story"? You can be as creative or as literal as you like: The Black Hole Story, The Big Mistake Story, or The Lousy Marriage Story. For the next few weeks, as soon as you notice any feeling, thought, or memory connected with this story, simply name it: "Aha. Here's 'The Life Sucks Story' again!"

Next, having noticed and named the story, you gently refocus. You don't try to push the story away or distract yourself from it. Rather, you allow it to be present, just as in the exercise where you let it rest on your palm. And acknowledging the story is present, you expand your awareness: noticing where you are, what you're doing, what's going on, then focusing your attention on what you're doing.

It's important to do this with a sense of humor and playfulness. If you're unable to do that, skip this method, as without those elements it could backfire and hook you more. But if you *can* do it playfully, with a bit of lightness and humor, over time it should help you unhook more easily.

Of course, there will be times when you're hooked by the story before you even realize it. So the moment you notice, you name it: "Aha! Just got hooked by 'The No Hope Story' again."

EXERCISE: Singing the Story

1. Pick a nasty judgment about your partner (or yourself) and put it into a short sentence, no more than a few words long: "He's a pig!" or "I'm too selfish!"

2. Now silently sing it to the tune "Happy Birthday."

3. And now silently sing it to a tune of your choice.

What happened? Most people find the thought loses its power as they see it for what it is: a string of words, like the lyrics in a song. Those words, of course, may be true or false, exaggerated or realistic, harsh or fair—but that's not the point! The point is simply: they're words. Nothing more nor less than words popping up inside your head. Once we can see the true nature of a thought—that it's basically a string of words (sometimes accompanied by pictures)—it's usually easier to unhook.

EXERCISE: Hearing the Story in a Funny Voice

This exercise is the same as the previous one, except instead of singing it, you silently say the thought in a funny voice. For example, the voice of a movie star, sports commentator, or cartoon character. Do this with at least two or three different voices, and notice what happens.

The previous exercises are all useful tools for unhooking. However, if we compare them to "working out" at the gym, they are the equivalent of lifting light weights. And of course, lifting light weights is very useful; it helps you get fitter and stronger. But if you want to really build up those muscles, you'll need to progress to heavier weights. And so it is with our psychological muscles. If you want to excel at unhooking, you'll need to practice more challenging exercises. The following exercises are harder than the previous ones, but the rewards for doing them are much greater.

TWO EXERCISES: Hearing or Seeing Your Thoughts

The next two exercises—"Hearing Your Thoughts" and "Leaves on a Stream"—both require you to use my free audios, which you'll find in chapter 9 of "Extra Bits." (Final reminder: This free e-book is download-able from the free resources page of thehappinesstrap.com.) The "Hearing Your Thoughts" audio guides you through an exercise where you listen in to what your mind is saying—as if listening to an interview on the radio. It helps you notice where that "voice inside your head" is located and the speed, rhythm, volume, pitch, and emotional tone of the words.

The "Leaves on a Stream" audio guides you through seeing, watch-ing, or visualizing your thoughts. You imagine you're sitting by the side of a gently flowing stream, and there are leaves floating on the surface. As thoughts pop into your head, you place them on leaves and let them float on by.

Please choose one of these exercises—whichever you prefer—and practice it for five to ten minutes two or three times a week. (The more practice the better, but even once a week is better than nothing.) Practicing either exercise on a regular basis will help you develop a very important skill: how to observe your thought stream without getting pulled into it; how to let them freely come and stay and go, without getting hooked. This skill is a powerful antidote to worrying, ruminating, and obsessing, which all involve the opposite: getting pulled into the stream of your thoughts.

EXERCISE: Dipping In and Out of the Stream

This final exercise—a modification of dropping anchor—takes about six or seven minutes. (And the easiest, most effective way to do it is to use the free audio in chapter 9 of "Extra Bits" and let my voice guide you.)

When we ruminate, worry, or obsess, we get "carried away" by the stream of our thoughts. In this exercise, we repeatedly "dip in and out" of that thought stream. We recognize when the stream has carried us off, and we "pull ourselves out of it." Part A is easier: dipping in and out of pleasant thoughts. Part B—dipping in and out of uncomfortable thoughts—is more challenging, but absolutely essential. Why? Because when we are worrying, ruminating, or obsessing, we *are* lost in a stream of unpleasant thoughts—so we need to learn how to get out of it.

If you choose not to use the free audio, follow the written instructions. Read them through once so you know what's involved, then go back to the start and follow them, step by step. (In this case, you'll require some sort of timer.)

Part A: Dipping In and Out of a Pleasant Stream

Step 1: Set your timer for thirty seconds, and start it. Then immediately begin daydreaming, imagining, or fantasizing about something very pleasant and enjoyable. Get thoroughly absorbed in these pleasant thoughts.

Step 2: When the alarm rings (after thirty seconds), drop anchor for fifteen to thirty seconds. As you do this, make sure you acknowledge the thoughts and feelings present (remember, this isn't distraction). For example, silently say, "Here are some pleasant thoughts" or "I'm noticing an enjoyable fantasy." Once anchored, recognize you have a choice: to jump back into the stream *or* to focus your attention fully on what you're doing.

Step 3: Again, set the timer for thirty seconds and start it. Then plunge back into that stream of enjoyable thoughts, and let it sweep you away.

Step 4: When the timer rings, drop anchor for fifteen to thirty seconds. Then once again, acknowledge your choice point: go back into the stream or engage in your life.

Step 5: For one last time, set the timer, dive back into your stream of pleasant thoughts, and stay there for thirty seconds.

Step 6: When the alarm goes, again drop anchor for fifteen to thirty seconds. Refocus on where you are and what you're doing.

Part B: Dipping In and Out of an Unpleasant Stream

Part B is more challenging, but essential. It's the same as part A, except now you worry, ruminate, or obsess.

Step 1: Recall something you worry, ruminate, or obsess about, and again, set the timer for thirty seconds. Start the timer, and get as hooked as possible: for half a minute, worry, ruminate, or obsess as much as you can.

Step 2: When the alarm goes, drop anchor for fifteen to thirty seconds. Remember: this is *not* distraction, so it's essential to acknowledge the thoughts and feelings present. For example, silently say to yourself, "Here's anxiety" or "I'm noticing scary thoughts." Once anchored, acknowledge your choice point: jump back into that stream or give your full attention to what you're doing.

Step 3: Reset the timer for thirty seconds, and start it. Then lose yourself in the stream for thirty seconds: worry, obsess, or ruminate away.

Step 4: When the alarm goes, drop anchor for fifteen to thirty seconds. Acknowledge your options: plunge back into your thoughts or focus on where you are and what you're doing.

Step 5: For one last time, set the timer, start it, dive back into the stream, and immerse yourself in those thoughts for half a minute.

Step 6: When the timer rings, again drop anchor for fifteen to thirty seconds. Refocus on where you are and what you're doing. Be fully present in your life.

So how did you do? Most people find that initially it's quite hard to leave the stream—and sometimes they don't even want to leave it! And isn't that what it's like when we go through the day, worrying, ruminating, and obsessing? Even though we know it's not helpful, we feel the pull to keep doing it. Hopefully, however, you found by the end of the exercise that it was getting easier to unhook and refocus. If not, try it again, and this time work harder at dropping anchor; notice and name your difficult thoughts and feelings (so this doesn't turn into distraction) while also moving your body and refocusing attention.

Apply this skill repeatedly throughout the day: as soon as you realize you're inside-the-mind, lost in the smog, worrying, ruminating, obsessing. Drop anchor for fifteen to thirty seconds, then acknowledge your choice: you can go back into your thought stream or you can focus attention on what you're doing.

***

Well, we've now spent three whole chapters on unhooking from thoughts. So how do we unhook from feelings? I'm glad you asked…

CHAPTER 10

Hooked on a Feeling

Enough about thoughts, already! Let's talk about feelings. When your partner insults you, or forgets your anniversary, or embarrasses you in public, or says something that cuts you to the quick, or stays out all night and comes home drunk, or leaves clothes lying all over the house, or promises to come home early but doesn't, or makes an important decision without consulting you, or does zillions of other things that push your buttons: at times like these, painful feelings are inevitable—anger, sadness, anxiety, frustration, disappointment, you name it.

And as discussed earlier, when painful feelings show up, we have two common modes of responding. In OBEY mode, we're on autopilot: highly reactive, with little self-awareness or self-control; our feelings dictate the things we say and do.

In STRUGGLE mode, we try hard to avoid or get rid of these unwanted thoughts and feelings: drugs, alcohol, comfort food, distraction, positive thinking, procrastination, avoiding unpleasant situations, and so on. And as discussed earlier, there are three main problems with this way of responding:

1. Although these methods work quite well when emotional pain is mild, they're usually ineffective when feelings are intense.

2. Any relief obtained is usually brief; those painful feelings quickly return.

3. When used excessively or inappropriately, these methods create new problems, which then give rise to even more painful feelings.

It's far more effective to respond to difficult feelings with *unhooking*. And so far we've covered two methods for doing this: *dropping anchor* and *notice, name, refocus*. These methods work with any inner experience: thoughts, feelings, sensations, urges, images, or memories. (We always modify the "naming" to match the experience: *I'm noticing feelings of sadness; here's an urge to drink; here's anger; I'm noticing tightness in my chest; I'm having a feeling of anxiety.*) However, when intense, painful emotions are hanging around, we often need additional ways of unhooking. I collectively refer to these methods as "making room."

When painful feelings appear, we tend to tighten up around them. Rather than "give them room," we try to squeeze them out or squash them down or push them away. This is like locking an angry horse inside a small tin shed. The horse will pound its hooves against the sides, hammering away, frantic to escape—and in the process, do a lot of damage. But suppose you release that horse into a large open field. There it can run around to its heart's content. Soon it will expend all its energy and settle down. In much the same way, we can learn to open up around strong feelings. If we give them plenty of room, they can expend their energy without hooking us.

Shortly you'll learn how to do this. But first, let's...

Get Clear on Your Motivation

In a moment, you're going to deliberately contact an uncomfortable emotion and practice making room. But why? What matters enough that you'd be willing to do that? If you're doing it primarily because you want to feel better, happier, calmer—or to stop you feeling anxious, sad, or angry—then you're setting yourself up for disappointment. We know, in the long term, you *will* feel a lot better with the ACT approach to life—more than three thousand scientific studies confirm this—but if your primary aim is "to feel good," then you're right back in STRUGGLE mode.

The reason you're learning to make room for painful emotions is to enable you to choose more toward moves, help you behave like the person you want to be, and empower you to do things that make your relationship better. As you know, when hooked, we tend to do away moves. But when we're unhooked, it's easier to connect with our values and do things that take us toward the life we want. So ask yourself, if you were better at unhooking from these painful emotions...

- What values would you bring more into your relationship?

- What would you say or do differently in your relationship?

- How would you treat yourself differently?

- How would you treat your partner differently?

Please consider this carefully, then write a few sentences in answer to this question: *I am going to learn this new skill of "making room" for my emotions, so that I can do important toward moves such as....*

How to TAME Your Emotions

TAME is an acronym for the four steps involved in this next exercise:

T: Take note (notice and name what's showing up in your body)

A: Allow (give your feeling permission to be there; "let it be")

M: Make room (open up around this feeling, and let it freely flow through you; let it come and stay and go in its own good time)

E: Expand awareness (continue to acknowledge your feeling, while broadening your focus to include the world around you)

This exercise is quite similar to dropping anchor. The main difference is the "make room" component, where we go beyond acknowledging and allowing these feelings, to actively "opening up" around them.

After you've done the exercise several times, it's good to create your own version by mixing, matching, and modifying the various components; once you know what they are, you can assemble them in any sequence you want (and leave out any you dislike).

The best way to do this exercise is to use the free audio in "Extra Bits" and let my voice guide you through it. If that doesn't suit, you can use the written instructions—but please read them through *at least twice* before you attempt this. (When you see a row of dots, that means pause for three to five seconds.) And if there's any part of the exercise you can't do, skip it and move on to the next part; there's no one component that's essential.

Preparing Yourself

Before we start this exercise, a few practical tips to fully prepare:

1. **Start small and scale up.** You can practice "making room" for any sort of emotion, urge, or sensation, no matter how great or small. So it's wise to start with smaller, not-too-difficult emotions, then build up your "psychological muscles" over time, progressively working with bigger, more challenging feelings.

2. **There's often more than one feeling present.** Painful feelings like company. So in the *Take note* component, notice and name all the feelings present. E.g., *I'm noticing sadness, anger, and fear.* Then focus your attention on whichever feeling is most prominent or whichever part of the body you feel it most.

3. **Don't expect your mind to be helpful.** Your mind is likely to say unhelpful things: *It's too hard, I hate these feelings, I can't handle them, what's wrong with me for feeling this way, I should be stronger than this, I shouldn't have to do this,* and so on. If any such thought hooks you, you know what to do: notice it, name it, and refocus on the exercise.

4. **Be ready to drop anchor (if needed).** I'm not expecting your feelings to overwhelm you—but if that were to happen, dropping anchor is your best immediate response. Once anchored, make a choice: continue the exercise from where you left off or leave it for now and try again later with something not so challenging.

So, if you're clear on your motivation, and you've prepared yourself as previously described, let's TAME an emotion.

EXERCISE: TAME an Emotion

Get yourself into a comfortable position, and either close your eyes or fix them on a spot in front of you. And think about a problem in your relationship for long enough to bring up a difficult feeling. (Any emotion will do. You can practice your "making room" skills with any feeling—anger, sadness, anxiety, loneliness, and even with feelings of numbness.) Once a difficult feeling is present...

1. Take Note

Part A: Notice what you're doing. With genuine curiosity, notice how you are sitting...notice your feet on the floor...the position of your back... where your hands are, and what they are touching...

And whether your eyes are open or closed, notice what you can see...and notice what you can hear...and smell...and taste...

And notice what you are thinking...and feeling...and doing...

Part B: Notice your body. Now quickly scan your body from head to toe. Start at your scalp and move downward...

Notice the sensations you can feel in your head...face...jaws... throat...neck...shoulders...chest...upper arms...forearms...hands...abdomen...pelvis and buttocks...thighs...lower legs...and feet.

Part C: Notice your feeling. Now zoom in on the part of your body where the feeling is most intense. Observe that feeling closely, as if you're a curious child who's found something fascinating...

(At times, your thoughts may hook you and pull you out of the exercise. The moment you notice this, name it: *Just got hooked.* Then refocus your attention on the task.)

Notice where this sensation starts and stops...Learn as much about it as you can...

If you drew an outline around it, what shape would it have?...Is it two-dimensional or three-dimensional? On the surface of the body or inside you, or both?...How far inside you does it go?...Where is it most intense?...Where is it weakest?...

Observe it with curiosity...How is it different in the center than around the edges? Is there any pulsation or vibration within it?...Is it light or heavy?...Moving or still?...What is its temperature?...Are there any hot spots or cold spots?...

Notice the different elements within it...

Notice that it's not just one sensation; there are sensations within sensations...

Notice all the different layers to it...

Part D: Name the feeling. Take a moment to name this feeling...

Silently say to yourself, "I'm noticing a feeling of XYZ." If you don't know what to name it, "pain," "hurt," or "discomfort" will do.

2. Allow

See if you can allow this feeling to be there.

You don't have to like it or want it; just allow it...

Just let it be...

Silently say: "I don't like or want this feeling, but I will allow it." Or simply state the word "allowing."

You might feel a strong urge to fight with it or push the feeling away. If so, acknowledge the urge is there without acting on it. And continue observing the sensation...

Don't try to get rid of it or alter it. Your aim is simply to allow it...to let it be...

3. Make Room

Part A: Breathe into it. And as you're noticing this feeling, breathe into it...

Imagine your breath flowing into and around this feeling...

Get a sense of breathing into and around it...

Part B: Expand around it. And it's as if, in some magical way, all this space opens up inside you...

You open up around this feeling...

Make space for it...

Expand around it... (You're aiming to get a sense of opening up around the feeling instead of squeezing in on it. It's often helpful to tense up all the muscles around this spot and then slowly ease off the tension.)

Breathing into it...opening up...expanding around it...

And as you continue to observe this feeling, see if there's anything underneath it. For example, if anger or numbness is at the surface, perhaps underneath it is fear, sadness, or shame.

Don't try to make a new feeling appear: if a new one emerges, that's okay; if it doesn't, that's okay too. Whatever feeling is present in this moment, let it have its space...

Part C: Sense it as an object. Get a sense of this feeling as if it were a physical object (you don't have to visualize it; just sense its physical properties)...

As an object, what shape and size does it have?...

Does it seem to be liquid, solid, or gaseous?...

Is it moving or still?...

If you could touch the surface, what would it feel like?...Wet or dry? Rough or smooth? Hot or cold? Soft or hard?...

Get a sense of this "object" inside you and observe it from all sides...

If you like visualizing, imagine its color...whether it's transparent or opaque...

Curiously observe this object. Breathe into it, and open up around it...

You don't have to like it or want it. Just allow it...

4. Expand Awareness

Continue to notice your feeling...and as you're doing so, expand your awareness to notice other parts of your body...

Notice your arms and legs and head and neck...

And notice that you're in control of your arms and legs, regardless of what you're feeling; move them around to check this out for yourself...

Now take a stretch, and notice yourself stretching...

And also notice the room around you...

Open your eyes, look around, and notice what you can see...and notice what you can hear...and breathe in the air, noticing what you smell...

And reach out and touch some things around you (like your chair, or your clothes, or this book)...

And notice there's so much more here than your feelings...your feelings are inside a body, which is inside a room, where you are working to develop an important skill, in the service of building a better relationship...

And now it's time to end this exercise by focusing your full attention on whatever activity you are doing.

So, now that you've read the instructions, please do the exercise, step by step. (Or better still, use the audio.) And if you're not keen on a particular component (e.g., breathing around the feeling, or visualizing its color), skip that bit. (However, I do encourage you to try every component at least once.)

Ready to try it for real? Off you go!

So how did you do? Hopefully, as you made room for the feeling, you had a sense of unhooking: it lost some of its impact; it was easier to have it around; you were no longer compelled to OBEY or STRUGGLE; you gained control over your arms and legs.

If you found it hard to do, you're not alone. For most people, it's a brand-new skill. And it's very challenging, because it's so radically different to all those STRUGGLE strategies we normally use. But, like any new skill, it improves with practice. (And if you had major difficulties, please read the troubleshooting section in "Extra Bits.")

Keep in mind, that was a *long* exercise; you can easily create shorter versions. You can take any individual component and turn it into a sixty-second exercise. Or you can combine two or three components into a two- to three-minute exercise.

Another thing that can help is some kind and caring self-talk. For example, you might silently remind yourself:

"This emotion is normal; it's a natural reaction to a difficult situation."

"Emotions are like waves: they rise and they peak and they fall."

"I'm willing to make room for this feeling, even though I don't like it."

"I don't have to let it control me; I can have this feeling and choose to do toward moves."

"Like all feelings, this will come and stay and go in its own good time."

Back to the "P" Word

Yup, it's time to use the "p" word once again: the more you *practice* these skills, the greater the benefits. "But," I hear you protest, "I can't do all that in the middle of an argument." You're dead right. Initially, you'll need to practice these skills in your own space and time. For example, you can do ultra-brief versions of TAME whenever you have a spare minute: in traffic jams, in supermarket lines, during a commercial break on TV, and so on. And if you're at home, and you're feeling all worked up, then you can take a bit longer, practice in more depth.

Over time, with repeated practice, you *will* be able to do this in an argument. You'll be able to notice your emotional storm building, and drop anchor before you get swept away. Your partner will say something provocative or hostile, and a flood of feelings will surge through your body: hurt, anger, fear, frustration, or despair. But you will be able to drop anchor, make room, and stay present.

On the other hand, if you're too worked up to talk things through reasonably, then you can call "time-out": leave the conflict, go to a different room, and run through TAME until you calm down. Then, when you're calm enough to talk in a way that's effective—using the skills we'll cover in later chapters—you can continue the discussion. In chapter 13, we'll explore the constructive use of "time-out" in a lot more detail.

Naturally, there will be times you forget to do this. You'll get hooked by your emotions before you realize it, and pulled into a destructive confrontation. That's part of being human. But even when that happens, you can practice TAME *after* the quarrel is over. This is far healthier than walking away, lost in your psychological smog, uselessly stewing over what your partner said and did.

But wait, there's more! In addition to everything just described, it's often powerful to add in a bit of...

Self-Kindness

When we're hurting badly, most of us are not particularly kind to ourselves. We often talk to ourselves harshly: *Don't be so weak. Suck it up. Get on with it. You're being pathetic. Other people have real problems; what have you got to complain about? You brought this on yourself. You deserve it. Stop whining. It's no big deal.* Or we turn to substances like drugs, alcohol, cigarettes, or junk food, attempting to push our pain away. But while these strategies offer short-term relief, they are not kind ways of treating our body. Indeed, many of the things we do when we're in STRUGGLE mode are majorly lacking in kindness.

If, however, we can acknowledge our pain and treat ourselves with kindness, we will handle those difficult feelings a whole lot better. Now some people react negatively to this idea: they see self-kindness as a sign of weakness, or falsely equate it to self-pity, or dismiss it as "airy-fairy," or say they "don't have time for it" because they've got "real problems to deal with." And on top of all that, men sometimes look down on it as "effeminate." But almost always, beneath these objections, there's a harsh double standard at play.

You see, when someone we love or care about is going through a tough time, we instinctively reach out to them in kind, caring, supportive ways. We see they're suffering and we want to help, so we treat them with kindness and consideration. And mostly we don't even think about it; it just comes naturally. But when *we* are struggling, suffering, hurting, we often withhold such basic kindness from ourselves. This is unfortunate, because not only does self-kindness help us unhook from painful emotions, but it also makes us stronger, healthier, and more resilient. In addition, it makes us more likely to face up to our problems and take action. How do I know all this? Because there are *hundreds* of scientific studies on this topic. However, in all of those published scientific papers, they don't use the term "self-kindness"; they call it...

Self-Compassion

I tend to avoid the term "self-compassion" because many people erroneously consider that to be a religious practice. Rest assured, it's not. While most religions do include such practices, self-compassion is firmly in the realm of modern science and taught by psychologists around the globe. There are many different definitions of self-compassion, but they all boil down to this: *acknowledge your pain, and respond with kindness.*

Sounds simple, doesn't it? Yet many people find it hard to do. Dr. Kristin Neff, a psychology professor at the University of Texas, has researched this topic extensively (Neff 2003). She sees self-compassion in terms of three core elements. Let's go through them.

Kindness. As we go through life, we will all screw up and make mistakes. We will get caught up in unhelpful beliefs. No matter how much we develop our unhooking skills, there will be times when we forget to use them. We will act in self-defeating ways, and we will hurt the very people we love the most. At times, we will feel inadequate, stupid, foolish, unlovable, or numerous other versions of "I'm not good enough." Naturally, this hurts. And we hurt even more when our partner mistreats or neglects us.

Wouldn't it be great if, during those times of suffering, you could reach out to someone who unconditionally accepts you? Someone who sees you as you are, with all your human foibles and flaws and weaknesses, but does not judge or condemn or criticize you? Someone who basically says, "Hey, I'm here for you. Let me help. I can see you're in pain. You're hurting. Whatever you need, I'm here for you"? Self-compassion means reaching out to yourself with caring, warmth, support, and understanding. It's an act of great kindness.

Common humanity. Often when you're suffering, your mind tells you that you are the only one suffering, that everybody else out there is happier than you are, that others don't feel as much pain as you, that others don't screw up or fail as much as you do. But if you clutch this story tightly, it will only make your suffering worse. If you're feeling guilty, fearful, angry, inadequate, lonely, ashamed, or resentful, it can be helpful to remember these are all normal human experiences. All over the planet, in this moment, there are millions upon millions of other humans suffering in ways very similar to your own.

The reality is all humans suffer. Not all to the same degree, of course. Poverty-stricken children growing up in war-torn third-world countries are likely to suffer much more than Western kids growing up in wealthy middle-class suburbia. But that's not the point. The point is to recognize you are human. Every human life will be touched by loss, rejection, failure, frustration, and disappointment. Every human being will lose their temper, screw up, or do things they regret. And every close, meaningful human relationship will at times have problems. To recognize this—and acknowledge how much you have in common with the rest of humanity—is an act of kindness in itself. It helps you realize you're not alone in your suffering, not weak or defective; you're normal, and this is part of being human.

Unhooking. You already know a lot about unhooking, and hopefully are practicing it more and more. (By the way, Neff doesn't use the term "unhooking"; she uses a different one, which I'll introduce in the next chapter.) When we drop anchor, make room for our painful feelings, loosen our grip on self-judgmental stories, step out of the smog, and focus our attention on what we're doing right here and now: these are all acts of self-kindness.

EXERCISES: Self-Compassion

Here are some strategies for developing self-compassion: ways to acknowledge your pain and respond with kindness.

The "Kind Hand"

(There's an audio for this in "Extra Bits." I strongly encourage you to use it; it's much more powerful than following the written instructions.)

1. First take a moment to acknowledge your pain: to notice and name whatever painful feelings are showing up.

2. Next, pick one of your hands and turn it palm up. At times you've used this hand in kind ways: to help out a friend with a task; to comfort a crying baby; to mop a fevered brow; to hold the hand or pat the back or rub the shoulders of a loved one who is frightened or hurting. Tap into that kindness, and imagine it filling up your hand.

3. Now locate the area of greatest pain in your body, and gently place your "kind hand" on top of it. (Or let your hand hover just above the surface.) Alternatively, place your hand on your heart.

4. Now send warmth and kindness from your hand into your body. Imagine, feel, or sense that warmth and kindness flowing into and around the pain, softening and loosening up around it.

5. Hold the pain gently, as if it's a frightened puppy or a crying baby. Send warmth and kindness up and down your body in all directions.

Kind Self-Talk

Suppose someone you love were suffering in a manner similar to yours. If you wanted to reach out to them with kindness, caring, and understanding, what would you say to them? There are three key ideas it's especially helpful to communicate:

- *I see you're suffering.*

- *I care about you.*

- *I'm here for you.*

How would you put these ideas into your own words? Take a couple of minutes to really think this through.

Now try saying something similar to yourself. If you're stuck for ideas, here are some phrases that many people find helpful:

This really hurts. Be kind to yourself.

This is hard. I'm doing my best.

I'm a fallible human being. We all make mistakes.

I screwed up. But, hey, I'm human. I can learn from this.

Alternatively, you may prefer this one, from Kristin Neff:

This is a moment of suffering; may I be kind to myself.

And if your mind's beating you up for screwing up, making mistakes, doing something you regret, then a phrase like this is often useful:

I'm a human being. Like everybody else on the planet, I am imperfect. We all make mistakes.

Last but not least, it's often helpful to remind yourself of this (putting it into your own words):

I'm a living, caring human being. And these painful feelings are something I have in common with every living, caring human on the planet. They are not a sign of weakness or defectiveness. They're a sign that I care; that I have a heart; that things matter to me! This is what all humans feel when there's a big gap between what we want and what we've got.

Kind Deeds

If a loved one were suffering in ways similar to yours, what kind deeds would you do for them? What actions would you take to support them? What gestures would you make to help, comfort, or care for them?

Now consider: What similar kind deeds can you do for yourself? This might involve anything from spending time with people who treat you

well, doing a sport or creative pursuit you enjoy, seeing a coach or therapist, practicing your unhooking skills, cooking healthy food, having a hot
bath or shower, getting a massage, listening to music you love, and so
on.

No matter how good your relationship gets, there will be times when
painful emotions arise. The better you are at supporting yourself, with
genuine kindness and consideration, the better you'll get through these difficult times. So practice this often. When your mind's beating you up,
unhook from the story and start speaking kindly to yourself. When painful
feelings show up, add a "kind hand" to your TAME. When life's getting you
down, do genuinely kind things for yourself. Self-compassion won't magically solve your problems, but it will help you cope better when you're deeply
hurting.

What Next?

So you've dropped anchor, emerged from the smog, made room for your feelings, treated yourself kindly, and refocused on what you're doing. What
next? Well, now you connect with your values and use them to guide your
actions. In some instances, that will involve using the new skills you'll learn
in chapters 14 to 16: communication, assertiveness, and negotiation. In
other instances, it could involve, well, just about anything; the number of
ways we can act on our values is vast. So on a daily basis, ask yourself,
"What values can I 'sprinkle' into my relationship today? What can I say or
do that might make it better?" Your values-guided actions may include anything from saying you're sorry to putting out the garbage, from buying
flowers to making the bed, from sharing a funny story to snuggling up in
bed, from offering to wash up to giving a massage, from asking "How was
your day?" to saying "I love you." Be creative, and notice what happens.

CHAPTER 11

Look at Me! Look at Me!

It's a sunny afternoon in the park. The little girl squeals excitedly as she cycles off down the hill. She lets go of the handlebars, lifts her arms high into the air. "Look at me! Look at me!" she yells. Her mother watches, smiling from ear to ear.

A young couple sits at a candlelit table. "You have amazing eyes," he says, gently holding her hand.

"Really?" she replies.

He nods, silently. As they gaze dreamily into each other's eyes, they are oblivious to everyone else in the restaurant.

The Gift of Full Attention

One of the greatest compliments you can pay another human is to give them your full attention. When you make someone the center of your attention, they feel important, cared about. They know they matter to you. And the reverse is also true. When someone is genuinely interested in you, feels pretty good, doesn't it?

Think of someone you greatly admire: your favorite movie star, athlete, author, rock star, or world leader—someone you'd love to meet in your wildest fantasies. Now suppose that person suddenly walked into the room. Would you give them your full attention? Absolutely! You'd "drink them in." You'd notice what they were wearing, how they were looking, what they were doing. And you'd listen with great interest when they were talking. You'd take note of their facial expressions, you'd register their tone of voice. You'd be keen to get their opinion, and you'd reflect carefully on whatever they had to say. And if they had some odd quirks to their personality, you wouldn't judge them harshly; you'd accept it as an eccentricity. You certainly wouldn't get upset about it or take it personally. And you'd probably feel some nerves or anxiety—as we often do in the presence of those we admire—but you'd willingly make room for those feelings to spend some time with this person.

In this scenario, you are paying full attention; you are interested, engaged, fully present, and open to your experience. In other words, you're being *mindful*. I've avoided the word "mindfulness" until now because there are so many popular misconceptions about it. For example, people often mistakenly believe that mindfulness is a type of meditation. Or a religious practice. Or a relaxation technique. Or a type of positive thinking. Or a way to control your feelings. Or a method for "emptying your mind." But "mindfulness" is none of these things. So what *is* it?

There are many definitions of mindfulness floating about, but if you put them all together, and strip them down to basics, you get this: *"Mindfulness" is a set of psychological skills for effective living, which all involve paying attention with openness, curiosity, and flexibility.*

When we notice and name, drop anchor, dip in and out of the stream, emerge from the psychological smog, make room for difficult feelings, expand awareness, and engage in an activity, those are all *mindfulness* practices. I've been calling them *unhooking* skills to get away from all those popular misunderstandings about mindfulness. (So in the previous chapter, when I mentioned Neff's formula for self-compassion, the terms she actually uses are kindness, common humanity, and *mindfulness*.)

Not only do thoughts and feelings hook our actions and pull us into doing those away moves, but they also hook our attention and pull it away from where it's most needed. So our unhooking skills not only help us control our actions, but also refocus our attention on what's most important in this moment. And central to all the unhooking (or mindfulness) skills we've covered is a particular way of paying attention: with *openness, curiosity*, and *flexibility*. As we notice, name, allow, and make room, that's openness—the very opposite of STRUGGLE. And every skill emphasizes curiosity, because even if something is very difficult or unpleasant, if we are genuinely curious, we can learn something useful: either about its true nature or about how to respond to it more effectively.

In addition to openness and curiosity, all those unhooking exercises encourage flexibility of attention. Think of your life as an ever-changing stage show. On that stage are all your thoughts and feelings, and everything you can see, hear, touch, taste, and smell. And there's a part of you that can zoom in and out of that show, lighting up any aspect at any time. Sometimes you illuminate your thoughts, or you put a particular emotion in the spotlight. At other times, you shine a light on the world around you: all those things you can see, hear, touch, taste, and smell. At times you may zoom in to one part of the show, so you can take in all the intimate details. At other times, you may zoom out, lighting up the whole stage to "get the big picture."

All of this involves "flexible attention": the ability to narrow, broaden, sustain, or shift your focus, depending on what's most useful in this moment. If you wish to walk mindfully through the countryside and take in all the sights, sounds, and smells, then that requires a broad focus of attention, which shifts from moment to moment. In contrast, if you're a neurosurgeon, mindfully operating on a tiny part of the brain, then you want to fix and sustain a very narrow focus for a long time.

In the ACT model, all these unhooking or mindfulness skills serve the same purpose: they help us unhook from our thoughts and feelings and focus our attention on what we're doing, so we can act on our values and get more fulfillment out of life. And I'm sure you've noticed that there's nothing religious about any of the practices we've covered; no meditation; no positive thinking; and no attempts to relax, "empty your mind," or control your feelings.

Of course, as we do these practices, uncomfortable emotions often reduce, and difficult thoughts *do* often disappear, and feelings of relaxation *do* often arise; however, these are "lucky bonuses," not the main aim. If you use your new skills to deliberately try to achieve such outcomes, then you're no longer practicing mindfulness; you've fallen back into STRUGGLE mode, trying to avoid or get rid of unwanted thoughts and feelings. In which case, you'll soon be disappointed and complain that *this doesn't work!*

Why Attention Wanes

In the early days of your relationship, you and your partner were probably both attentive to and curious about each other, and very much "present." Then, over time, the magic wore off. And there's nothing abnormal about that—it happens to all of us. And here's why:

Your mind paints a portrait of your partner, and then mistakes that painting for the real person. But a painting is static; it doesn't change. And after a while, you know every detail of that painting. Heck, you've seen it a million times—and it's no masterpiece. So gradually you start to lose interest. You may still appreciate it, but it no longer captivates you. And so, bit by bit, the boredom creeps in. From time to time, you do stop to inspect it. But as time goes on, you seem to notice more and more flaws: the sloppy brushstrokes, the cracks in the canvas. And if you keep up this harsh, judgmental scrutiny, eventually you will start to detest this painting.

Many relationships travel down this road: from fascination to boredom to contempt. But it doesn't have to be that way. If that's the road you're on, you can rapidly turn around through practicing mindfulness. Instead of focusing attention on your thoughts, feelings, body, or the world around you—as in all the unhooking skills we've covered so far—you focus your full attention on your partner. You notice, with openness and curiosity, their face, lips, eyes, posture, and actions. You notice their tone of voice and the way they use words. You are genuinely curious about and open to their thoughts and feelings. You are intrigued by the way they see the world. Your partner now becomes your anchor; when you drift off into your thoughts, you catch yourself and refocus on your partner.

Mindfulness helps you separate the person from the painting. You realize there's far more depth to this person than any static portrait could ever capture. You begin to see the painting is a caricature: a few symbolic elements of this person, thrown together in a crude, cartoonish image. When you look at the painting closely, you see it's nothing but inanimate paint layered on canvas. But when you look at the real person, you discover the opposite: there you find depth, life, and meaning.

The word "engage" is derived from two French words: *en*, which means "make," and *gage*, which means "pledge." When you engage fully with your partner, you are making a pledge—one of friendship, caring, and love. At a level deeper than words, you are sending this message: *I see you, I care about you, I am here for you.*

Engaging with our partner is often hard. Why? Because our thoughts and feelings so easily hook our attention, and take it off somewhere else; we all repeatedly "drift off" and disconnect. So the exercises that follow are designed to build your "attention muscles," making it easier to be fully present with your partner.

The mindfulness exercises we've done so far all share a common format: first you pay attention to your thoughts or feelings, then you refocus your attention on your "here and now" experience: on where you are, or what's going on around you, or what you're doing in this moment. The following mindfulness exercises have a different format. In these practices, first you fix your attention on some aspect of your "here and now" experience; then you notice when your thoughts or feelings hook your attention; then you unhook from the thoughts or feelings that distracted you, and you bring your attention back to where it's required.

Exercises: Building Your "Attention Muscles"

In each exercise that follows, you'll focus your attention, *for one minute only*, on some aspect of your here and now experience—and if distracting thoughts and feelings arise, you:

1. Let them come and go like passing cars, and keep your attention on the task.

2. If hooked, gently acknowledge it, and refocus on the exercise.

Noticing the Environment

When you reach the end of this paragraph, put down the book and notice your surroundings. Notice as much as you can about what you can see, hear, touch, taste, and smell. What's the temperature? Is the air moving or still? What sort of light is there and where is it coming from? Notice five sounds you can hear, five objects you can see, and five things you can feel against the surface of your body (such as the clothes against your skin or the chair beneath you).

Please put the book down and do this for one whole minute. Notice what happens.

Noticing Your Body

As you're reading this paragraph, connect with your body. Notice where your legs and arms are and the position of your spine. Inwardly scan your body from head to toe; notice the sensations in your head, chest, arms, abdomen, legs. (And if there are parts of your body or sensations within it that you dislike, notice how you try to avoid them.)

Please put the book down and do this for one whole minute. Notice what happens.

Noticing Your Breath

As you're reading this, notice your breathing. Notice the rise and fall of your rib cage and the air moving in and out of your nostrils. Follow the air in through your nose. Notice how your lungs expand. Feel your abdomen push outward. Follow the air back out as the lungs deflate.

Please put down the book and do this for one whole minute. Notice what happens.

Noticing Sounds

If your hearing is not impaired, focus your attention on sounds. Notice sounds coming from you (e.g., from your breathing and your movements), sounds from the room around you, and sounds from outside.

Please put down the book and do this for one whole minute. Notice what happens.

So what did you notice? Hopefully, three things:

1. We are always in the midst of a sensory feast—but we often don't realize it.

2. Our thoughts and feelings easily hook our attention.

3. When we notice our attention has been hooked, we can quickly unhook and refocus.

Now as I've said a few times already (sorry for being repetitive), the key to learning new skills is to practice. If you only do those exercises once or twice, there'll be little or no benefit. So please practice them regularly. One option is to do thirty- to sixty-second versions (of any or all of them), as often as you can, throughout the day. Another option is to pick one or two of them and turn them into longer practices, lasting for at least several minutes; the longer they last, the more you'll build up those "attention muscles." If you're willing to try this second option, use the free audios in "Extra Bits" as a guide.

Going Further with Engagement

Let's now do some mindfulness exercises that involve focusing attention on your partner. (Inevitably, at times, you will get hooked while doing these. But you know what to do: notice and name what's hooking you, and refocus on your partner.)

Be mindful of expression. Notice your partner's facial expressions: notice how their eyebrows, forehead, and mouth are all involved. See if you can trace their emotions. Watch as if you had paid a small fortune to witness the performance of a great actor: what are they expressing with their face?

Be mindful of body language. Notice how your partner moves their body: their neck and shoulders, arms and legs, hands and feet. Watch the way they get into a car, climb the stairs, or walk down the hallway, as if you'd never seen them do this before. Notice the gestures their hands make when they talk. Notice how their posture changes with their emotions.

Be mindful of speech. Notice how your partner speaks: the rhythm and sound of their voice, the words they use, the speed and tempo, the emotional overtones.

Be mindful of emotions. Practice all of the previous steps simultaneously: notice your partner's face, body, and speech, all at once. Aim to tune into their emotions; to get a sense of what they may be feeling.

Cultivate curiosity and openness. When we talk, we like others to listen attentively. We like to know that they're interested and that they're open to hearing our thoughts and ideas, even if they don't agree with us. We don't feel good if the listener seems bored, distracted, hostile, critical, or dismissive. When interacting with your partner, you can cultivate curiosity and openness in several ways:

- Ask questions that help you to see the world from your partner's point of view, such as, "How do you feel about that?" or "What do you make of that?" or "What's your opinion?"

- When your partner speaks, listen as if your main aim is to make them feel important and cared about.

- Listen with the intention to learn: to discover what your partner is feeling and thinking, to discover more about how they see the world.

- Listen with the intention to connect: to interact and bond at a level deeper than words, to let them know that you are there and that you care.

- Unhook from unhelpful stories. You know the ones: *Here we go again—same old story. You don't know what you're talking about. I wish you'd just sort this out, and that's the end of it. I know exactly what you're going to say. I can't be bothered with this.* You can't stop your mind from generating such thoughts, but you can let them come and go like passing cars.

- To help with all of these efforts, you could pretend you're on a first date: you want to make a good impression, and get to know this person better. Ask questions and listen to their responses with the genuine intention of finding out more about them. Go on a voyage of discovery rather than assuming you already know them. *Remember:* the portrait is not the person. Take every opportunity to put the painting aside and meet the real human hidden behind it.

If Your Partner Is Willing

This exercise is a powerful way to help you and your partner engage mindfully with each other—but don't attempt it unless you are both 100 percent willing. If either partner does it *unwillingly*, it's highly likely to backfire.

EXERCISE: Mindful Cuddling

Cuddle up, hold hands, or gently hug each other for at least several minutes *without talking*.

Do this mindfully, as if you've never done it before.

Notice where your bodies connect and the feelings of warmth and pressure in those areas.

Notice the rhythms of your breathing.

Notice what you can feel underneath your fingers; notice what you can see, hear, and smell.

Let your thoughts come and go like passing cars, make room for your feelings, and focus your attention on the physical connection between you.

Generally five minutes is enough, but you can make it as short or as long as you like. Either partner can stop the exercise at any point by saying, with warmth and kindness, "Thank you. Can we take a break?"

Your aim is to create a deep connection, to be fully present with each other. You want your partner to sense, feel, and experience that they are the absolute center of your attention. (And each time you "drift off," notice and name what hooked you, and gently refocus.)

Afterward, discuss what happened. How did your mind hook you? What difficult feelings showed up? Did either of you try to disrupt the exercise—and if so, why? What did you learn that's relevant to improving your relationship?

Why Bother?

Why bother with all this hard work, when it's so much easier to switch off, half-listen, change the subject, or put forward your own opinions without taking account of your partner's? Well, for one thing, it's the antidote to boredom and disconnection. If you don't make the conscious effort to be curious, open, and attentive, you'll grow increasingly disinterested and dissatisfied with your partner—and vice versa.

Another excellent reason is that it's an essential first step in communication and negotiation; if you want to constructively address your issues, talk through your problems, and negotiate getting your needs met, you won't have much luck if you're not fully present: engaged, open, and curious. These are topics we'll get to very soon. But first, let's look at one more aspect of mindfulness. It's a simple but effective way to constructively influence the behavior of your partner, while also increasing your own satisfaction in the relationship. It's called...

CHAPTER 12

The Art of Appreciation

Child: (*pushing food away*) I don't want this.

Mother: (*angrily*) There are starving kids in Africa who don't get that much food in a whole year!

Child: So give it to them!

Did you ever have an encounter like this with your mother? I certainly did. Children are often unappreciative. But hey, adults aren't much better. How often do we truly appreciate what we have? There is so much that we take for granted. A few years back, a friend of mine developed cancer in his neck. He was cured, but the radiation therapy destroyed the salivary glands in his mouth, so now he has to chew gum all day long to produce enough saliva to keep his mouth moist. When did you last stop to appreciate your own saliva? It lubricates your mouth, moistens your food, helps you digest what you eat. Most of the time, we hardly notice its presence. But we sure notice its absence when our mouth goes dry!

And when did you last truly appreciate your immune system? All day long, it's busy wiping out bugs of all shapes and sizes to ensure we remain fit and healthy. Yet as long as our health is good, we take it for granted. It's only when we come down with a bug that we realize how good we usually have it. And how good do we feel when we finally recover from that bug? For maybe an entire day, or even two, we truly appreciate our health and well-being. But all too quickly, we take it for granted again.

And we do this with virtually every aspect of our life. We take our hands for granted—until they get injured. We take our memory for granted—until it falters. If we have good eyesight and hearing, we rarely think twice about it—until it's impaired. We repeatedly fail to appreciate just how much these things contribute to our quality of life.

Not so long ago, I was walking along a riverbank, and I was caught up in a story about getting old: "I used to be able to walk so much faster than this. And now my knees creak and my back aches. And I'm only fifty-six years old!" I didn't notice the ancient guy on his walking stick until he laughed loudly and said, "I wish I could walk as fast as you!" That literally stopped me in my tracks. I chuckled and went on my way with a different attitude, marveling at how well my legs were still carrying me after fifty-six years of pounding the planet.

So what's this got to do with relationships? Well, just about everything! How do you feel when you are ignored, dismissed, or taken for granted? We are all very similar under the skin. We all want to be acknowledged and appreciated. When others show appreciation, we feel valued; we feel as if our efforts are noticed and that we make a difference. And if they don't show appreciation, we feel, well, a whole range of things from irritation and disappointment to loneliness or sadness.

The word "appreciate" comes from the Latin words *ad* meaning "to" and *pretium* meaning "prize" or "value," so "appreciate" means "to value or prize something." No wonder we like to receive appreciation; how wonderful to be valued or prized by our partner! And our partner, of course, feels the same way.

So what would happen to your relationship if you showed your partner more appreciation? (As you reflect on this, see if your mind says anything unhelpful: *He'll just take me for granted. All I ever do is give. It'll never be enough for her. I shouldn't have to...?* If any such stories pop up, rest assured that's normal—but don't let them hook you.)

Appreciation is at the very heart of mindfulness. On automatic pilot, we do not appreciate what we have. But when we pay attention with openness and curiosity—when we consciously notice what we have, and actively appreciate it—we experience a sense of satisfaction and fulfillment. (Popular sayings such as "Stop and smell the roses" and "Count your blessings" point to this truth, but the problem is, we've heard them so often they tend to sound a bit corny.) Conversely, if we *don't* actively appreciate what we have, and instead get caught up in stories about what's missing, we experience a sense of lack and dissatisfaction.

Mindful Appreciation

The exercises that follow are designed to help you cultivate appreciation for things we all commonly take for granted. Please do them slowly, savoring the experience. (If you rush through them to reach the next chapter, then you've missed the whole point.)

EXERCISE: Mindful Tasting

Please first read through all the instructions, then put the book down and do the exercise.

Pick a small morsel of food, like a peanut or raisin or grape, or a small square of chocolate, or half a rice cracker. Close your eyes and place this food in your mouth. Let it rest on your tongue for a few moments, without chewing. Notice how your mouth salivates. Then chew the food as sloooowly as you can, noticing every taste and texture. Study the flavor as if you have never tasted anything like it. Savor it as if you haven't eaten for days.

Now take a moment to appreciate your tongue and your mouth. How much does the ability to eat, chew, and taste contribute to your life?

EXERCISES: Mindfulness with Appreciation

In the previous chapter, on page 130, there are four mindfulness exercises: noticing the environment, your breath, your body, and the sounds you can hear. Now please do these exercises again, but this time, with a *sense of appreciation*. Actively appreciate your ability to notice the environment through your senses; your ability to breathe the air; the fact you have a body, and all the amazing things it constantly does. (And finally, if your hearing is not impaired, appreciate your ability to take in the sounds around you.)

We're always in the midst of life's amazing and ever-changing stage show: our thoughts and feelings, and everything we can see, hear, touch, taste, and smell, all continually changing from moment to moment. And isn't it astounding that we are able to witness and interact with this show? In his book *The Miracle of Mindfulness*, Buddhist monk and Nobel Peace Prize nominee Thich Nhat Hanh (1976) writes, "The real miracle is not to walk on water or in thin air, but to walk on earth. Every day we are engaged in a miracle which we don't even recognize: a blue sky, white clouds, green leaves, the black, curious eyes of a child—our own two eyes. All is a miracle."

The Art of Appreciation

At times, appreciation happens spontaneously. But most of the time, we simply don't appreciate the magnificent ever-changing stage show of our life. Our mind creates a T-shirt with the slogan: "Been there! Done that! Seen the movie! Read the book!" Then it pulls that T-shirt over our head and leaves it there.

Mindfulness is like peeling this T-shirt off so you can see the world with new eyes. If you use mindfulness to cultivate appreciation for your partner, both of you will benefit. The more you notice the many different ways your partner contributes to your life, the more satisfied you will feel in your relationship. And the more your partner feels appreciated, the more likely they are to respond with warmth and caring.

Many people, during periods of conflict and tension, fantasize about breaking up with their partner. But if it actually happens, it's usually a massive shock. Most people find breaking up from a serious, long-term relationship is extremely stressful. Indeed, on the brink of breaking up, one partner often starts to appreciate just how much the other contributes to their life. Why do we so often wait until the point of no return before we truly appreciate what our partner gives us? The answer: psychological smog. When you're trapped inside-the-mind, you can't appreciate what you have right in front of you.

Joe, an accountant, took his husband, Clem, for granted. Joe also judged Clem harshly for giving up his career in graphic design, and choosing instead to be a full-time homemaker. But all that changed when Clem got cancer. As Clem became sicker and Joe had to take over the role of home-maker—looking after the kids, maintaining the house, putting dinner on the table—he started to appreciate just how much Clem did for him and the family. Joe also began to recognize the million-and-one ways Clem enriched his life: the kisses, the conversation, the intimacy, the friendship, support, and love. Fortunately Clem survived, and their relationship grew much stronger through the experience. Many others are not so lucky. I've had numerous clients tell me that they only truly appreciated their partner once it was far too late. There's an old English proverb that points to this: "We never know the worth of water 'til the well runs dry."

Appreciating Your Partner

Following are a few suggestions to cultivate appreciation for your partner. (If you're hurting too badly to do this, you can leave this for later. But if you do intend to stay in this relationship, the sooner you start this, the better.)

- Each day, notice three things (at least) that you appreciate about your partner. They don't have to be big things; they can be tiny. It might be the way they smile, or the sound of their laughter, or the warmth of their body beside you in the bed.

- Contemplate what your partner adds to your life. Consider these questions: If my partner were seriously ill, at risk of dying, what would I tell them I appreciated most about them? If my partner left, what would I find hardest about living without them?

- Each day, notice three ways (at least) in which your partner contributes to your life. Again, they don't have to be big things; they can be tiny. It might be the simple fact that they go to work to earn money to help pay for some of the things you enjoy having. Or the simple pleasure of having someone to talk to over dinner. Or the feeling of added security you have when you're not alone.

- Think back to when you first met your partner: Which of their personal qualities did you find most attractive? Each day, notice three things (at least) your partner says or does that are representative of these qualities.

- At the end of each day, in your journal or using the worksheet from "Extra Bits," write about whatever you have noticed in these exercises.

Don't Just Appreciate: Say Something!

Appreciating your partner will add to your own fulfillment, but what about them? How will they know you appreciate them? Sure, they may notice some positive changes in you: perhaps you'll seem warmer, more open, more affectionate, or less grumpy and critical. But they may not have the slightest idea why. So why not tell them? You know how good it feels when someone acknowledges your contribution, so why not give that pleasure to your partner? Here are a few examples:

"I really appreciate the way you look after the house."

"Thank you for working so hard to help us have this lifestyle."

"I'm so glad you're in my life. Thank you for being here."

"I love feeling your body next to me in bed."

"I appreciate the efforts you're making with my parents. I know how hard it is for you."

"Thank you for doing ABC. I know it's not really your thing. It means a lot to me."

"I really enjoyed it last night when you did XYZ."

This may not come naturally at first, but it's well worth persisting until it does. And keep in mind, you can show appreciation without words. You might stroke or hug or kiss your partner; cook them a meal, buy them some flowers, or cook dinner. Words, however, are important. For most people, they carry a lot of weight. So don't avoid using them just because you feel awkward or uncomfortable.

Another thing: if your partner does start saying these sorts of things to you, make sure you respond positively. If your mind says, *They don't really mean that* or *They're just saying that because they read it in the book*, make sure to unhook. Don't make the same mistake as Ellie. When Vanessa started telling Ellie how much she appreciated her, Ellie completely undermined her. Ellie would say things like, "You sound so insincere. Say it like you mean it." But Vanessa *was* sincere. Vanessa's voice may have sounded odd because she was embarrassed. She was learning a new way to talk, and she felt uncomfortable—but she did mean every word she said. Sure enough, after a few of these put-downs from Ellie, Vanessa stopped trying. The moral of the story? If your partner makes the effort to appreciate you, then make sure that *you* appreciate their effort.

Carrot Versus Stick

Do you like carrots? Personally, I'm not too keen on them. But then, I'm not a donkey. Donkeys absolutely love carrots. So if you own a donkey, and you want it to carry heavy loads, what's the best way to motivate it? You guessed it: with carrots. Carry the load, and get a tasty snack. There is, however, an alternative method to motivate your donkey: you can whack it with a big wooden stick. Both methods will get your donkey moving—but over time, if you overuse the stick, your donkey will become a miserable, battered beast. In contrast, if you rely mostly on carrots, over time, you'll have a happy, healthy donkey.

When it comes to motivation, humans are not that different from donkeys. Did you ever have a coach, teacher, mentor, or parent who noticed the things you did right, commented on your improvements, and praised you for making progress? And did you ever have one who only noticed what you did wrong, and only commented on what wasn't good enough? How did the two compare with each other?

Unfortunately, in trying to motivate our partner, most of us use the stick far more than the carrot. And the stick comes in a wide variety of forms: judging, criticizing, blaming, threatening, shouting, withdrawing, giving the "silent treatment," and so on, and so on. These "sticks" may sometimes get your partner moving, but they'll damage your relationship in the long run.

Catch Them Doing It Right

No matter how much strife there is in your relationship, there are surely some things your partner does that you approve of. So see if you can "catch them doing it right." When they do something that you approve of, notice it, acknowledge it, and let them know you appreciate it. If you do this regularly, there's a good chance this behavior will increase. Why? Simply because humans like to be noticed, acknowledged, and appreciated by the people they care about, so they tend to do more of whatever makes this likely.

When a particular type of behavior increases over time because it gets you something that you want, psychologists call this "positive reinforcement." And if a particular type of behavior reduces over time, because you *lose* something you want or get something you *don't* want, psychologists refer to this as "punishment." Unfortunately, most of us try to influence our partner's behavior ineffectively, by trying hard to "punish" behavior we don't like. It's actually far more effective to focus our efforts on positive reinforcement: trying to increase the behaviors we approve of.

Many people react negatively to this idea. Because of our upbringing, it may seem to go against the grain. After all, most of us as children only got rewarded when we did things the way adults wanted. And if we didn't do it like Mom or Dad or the schoolteacher wanted us to do it, something most unpleasant often followed! So the idea of using carrots rather than sticks might at first seem somewhat odd; but it's based on a wealth of scientific evidence.

For many decades, psychologists have studied how to best influence the behavior of both children and adults, and the findings are always the same: if you want to influence behavior *constructively*, in a way that promotes health and well-being and maintains a good relationship, then you need to use way, way, waaaaaaaaaaay more carrot than stick. A whole lot more positive reinforcement than punishment. (As the ancient proverb goes: *you catch more flies with honey than with vinegar.*)

One of the world's leading researchers in this area is psychologist John Gottman. Gottman's research suggests that if you want to positively influence your partner's behavior, you'll need to praise them five times as much as you criticize. Yes, you read that correctly—*five* times more praise than criticism. Does this seem outrageous? It certainly did to Jed.

One of Yvonne and Jed's recurrent arguments was housework. Jed liked to keep the house spectacularly tidy. Yvonne liked a reasonably tidy house, but didn't share the same high standards as Jed. She had a tendency to leave books on the dining room table, shoes on the living room floor, coats on the backs of chairs, and unwashed dishes in the sink. This really got Jed's goat. "Why can't you just pick up after yourself?" he'd ask in an irritable voice. "It's not that hard. Why do you have to leave all this stuff lying around the place?"

"I don't notice it," Yvonne would protest.

"It's not that hard," Jed would snap. "Just open your eyes." Often when he got home from work, he'd wander around the house, tidying up Yvonne's mess, grumbling about how lazy she was. He was so caught up in the "lazy wife" story, he failed to appreciate the many ways that Yvonne *did* help out. When Yvonne put her shoes away eight times out of ten, Jed only noticed the two times she didn't. When Yvonne washed up two nights a week, Jed only noticed the five nights she didn't. When Yvonne occasionally pulled out the vacuum and cleaned the carpets, Jed merely thought, "It's about time she lifted a finger to help!"

Jed's strategy is extremely ineffective, for two main reasons:

1. By constantly focusing on what Yvonne does *not* do, he increases his own frustration and dissatisfaction.

2. The most effective way to get Yvonne to do more housework is to notice all those times that she *does* do it and to tell her (being genuine) how much he appreciates it. That will likely make her feel valued, and therefore motivated to do more of it in the future.

How did Jed feel when we discussed this? Not too happy:

Jed: But I shouldn't have to do all that! She should just do it naturally.

Russ: That's a common reaction. Did you notice the "should" there? Let me ask you, when you get hooked by "Yvonne should be tidier," what happens to your relationship?

Jed: It gets worse.

Russ: So here's the thing: your mind will tell you again and again and again, "Yvonne should be tidier." It's not likely to suddenly stop saying this, is it?

Jed: No, because it's true. She *should* be tidier.

Russ: Well, millions of people would agree with you. But the question is, when that thought shows up, is it helpful to get caught up in it? To dwell on it? Or let it dictate what you say and do?

Jed: No.

Russ: So what if you were to unhook from that story when it pops up: notice it, name it, refocus?

Jed: I don't feel like I can.

Russ: So check your experience: for ten years, you've been getting hooked by that story—has it brought you and Yvonne closer together?

Jed: No.

Russ: Has it changed Yvonne's behavior in any lasting way?

Jed: No.

Russ: So then, is it helpful for you to keep holding on to it so tightly?

Jed: I guess not. But it's hard to just let go of it, just like that.

Russ: Sure. Absolutely. This stuff is hard. You'll need to practice those unhooking skills over and over. So for the sake of your relationship, is it worth making the effort?

Jed: Well, when you put it like that—yes.

To unhook from all his "shoulds" was a huge challenge for Jed. Over the next few weeks, there were countless occasions where he wanted to criticize Yvonne and point out all the things she wasn't doing. But again and again, he dropped anchor, made room for his frustration, and in the service of his values, kept his mouth shut.

He also used the principle of positive reinforcement ("catch them doing it right"; "carrot versus stick"). When Yvonne hung up her coat (instead of flinging it on a chair), or washed the dishes, or made the bed, he'd thank her and tell her he appreciated it. Not surprisingly, over time, Yvonne's tidying behaviors gradually increased. Why? Well, first, she appreciated Jed's efforts to notice and acknowledge her contributions. That built some goodwill and motivated her to try harder. Second, the amount of fighting and tension decreased, which made her feel more warm and open—and therefore naturally more attentive to Jed's wishes. It's unlikely that Yvonne and Jed will ever have the same standards of tidiness and cleanliness. But they do have a better balance now. Yvonne is tidier than she was. Jed is more accepting than he was. It works better for both of them. It'll never be perfect—but then again, what is?

CHAPTER 13

Destructive Tactics

There are two types of couples in the world: those who fight, and those you don't know very well. Sometimes we meet a couple and they seem perfectly suited and blissfully happy, and we think, "Wow! Why can't my relationship be like theirs?" We get sucked right back into that "perfect partner" story. We forget that all we've seen is a tiny glimpse of this couple; we have no idea what they're like behind closed doors.

For all we know, they could be at each other's throats the moment they're home. We haven't a clue what they're like when they're sick or tired, or grumpy or bored or irritated. They might yell, shout, and scream at each other all night long. But our mind conveniently forgets this. Instead, it tells us that their relationship is wonderful, and there must be something wrong with our relationship because we have so much conflict.

Have you ever read about those fairy-tale marriages? Two rich, talented, sexy, beautiful movie stars tie the knot, and they seem so blissfully happy, so perfectly matched, so ecstatically in love. *A marriage made in heaven*, we think to ourselves. *They'll never fight and quarrel like we do, especially with all that wealth and luxury and glamour. What could they possibly fight about?* Then six months later, they divorce—and tell the whole world how awful their marriage was.

Now if you're prepared to completely straitjacket yourself, to suppress all your desires, put your life on hold, agree to your partner's every whim, and never protest or ask for what you want, then you may be able to get by without any conflict. But what would be the cost to you and your life? To have a healthy relationship, you need to honor your values, goals, rights, and needs—and the same goes for your partner. This means that at times you will have conflicting needs, desires, opinions, goals, attitudes, or interests. However, if we handle these conflicts constructively, with genuine caring and consideration for both ourself and our partner, then the relationship need not suffer. Damage only happens when one or both partners frequently resort to...

Using Destructive Tactics

At times, we all use "destructive tactics" either to get what we want or to avoid what we don't want (or both). I call them "destructive tactics" because although they often work in the short term, they destroy your relationship in the long term. They are radically different in nature to the healthy, constructive tactics we'll cover in the next few chapters. Let's look at the four main categories: attack, defend, detour, and withdraw.

1. Attack

Attack tactics all involve some degree of aggression. We may raise our voice; harshly judge or criticize; blame, shame, or call names; insult or put down. Or we may make threats: *I'm going to lose it in a moment! I'm warning you, I'm about to explode! If you don't stop, this relationship is over!* Attack tactics may include:

Springing the ambush: Your partner has done something that you don't like, but rather than address it, you hold on to it—sometimes for days or weeks. Then, in the heat of an argument, you unleash it, like pulling a concealed dagger from your sleeve.

Punching below the belt: Out comes the secret weapon. You know exactly what to say to play on your partner's deep-seated fears and insecurities. If their deepest fear is that you'll leave them, this is when you threaten divorce.

If they've been feeling sexually inadequate, this is when you tell them they're lousy in bed. Ouch! Ouch! Ouch!

Exhuming the corpse: This is when you dig up that rotting old corpse. Your partner did something a long time ago that hurt you badly. Although it's already long since dead and buried, you just won't allow it to rest in peace. Whenever you need some extra ammunition, you dig up the corpse and throw it in their face: "See? See what you did?"

2. Defend

Being defensive is the opposite of being considerate and responsible. We feel threatened by our partner's needs, opinions, or feelings. We don't try to see things from their perspective. We don't take responsibility for things we've said or done that they've found hurtful. Instead, we just defend ourselves against the perceived threat. (Of course, at times it's healthy and important to defend ourselves, and later we'll talk about how to do so in a caring, considerate manner.) Destructive defense tactics may include:

Pointing the finger: You start blaming your partner: "What about you? You did ABC," "This is your fault. If you hadn't XYZ, this would never have happened," "Why are you so needy?"

Playing the victim: You make yourself the victim: "Do you know hard this is for me?" "How do you think I feel?!" "And where does that leave me?"

Playing the lawyer: This is a favorite tactic of people with good debating skills. You twist your partner's words around, take them out of context, or exaggerate them to the point of ridicule.

3. Detour

There are many ways to detour around conflict with your partner. The most common is outright lying. But other tactics include doing things "behind your partner's back," concealing the truth, or saying things designed to mislead or deceive. Detour tactics may include:

Placating: To avoid or escape the conflict, you do what you can to appease or pacify your partner. You may give up on your needs, withdraw your requests, discount your rights, drop the topic, tell your partner whatever they want to hear, or go along with whatever your partner wants.

Gaslighting: This is an extremely toxic tactic, where one partner gets the other to doubt their own reality, memory, or perceptions. The gaslighting partner may falsely claim that they "don't know what you're talking about" or "can't recall the details." Or they may insist: "I've never said anything like that," "You're overreacting. It was nothing," "Why are you making a mountain out of a molehill?," "It didn't happen; you're imagining it," "You're being paranoid," "Your memory's playing tricks on you," "You're making things up."

4. Withdraw

Conflict of any sort brings up difficult feelings. To escape the conflict and all the painful emotions that go with it, many people withdraw. For example, they may storm out of the room, or stay but refuse to talk about the issue, or keep changing the topic. (Note: At times it *is* healthy and wise to take time-out from a conflict—but it needs to be done in a caring, considerate way, as we'll discuss shortly.) Withdrawal tactics can include:

Hiding away: You physically avoid your partner by staying in a different room, coming home late from work, or being "too busy" to find time for them.

The silent treatment: You go completely silent and refuse to talk.

The cold shoulder: You are deliberately cold and unfriendly toward your partner, maybe even ignoring them completely. You may even withhold affection or sex.

In a moment we'll explore why we use these tactics, but first let's address two very important points about withdrawal: 1) recognizing the "freeze response," and 2) the constructive use of "time-out."

RECOGNIZING THE FREEZE RESPONSE

When there's any sort of conflict with our partner, our "fight-or-flight" response instantly kicks in. This is an automatic, instinctive response, found in all mammals, birds, reptiles, and amphibians, and also in most types of fish. Basically, it's a response to a significant threat (whether the threat is real or merely perceived). Our nervous system recognizes the threat and prepares us physically for action, ready to either:

1. "Fight": Counterattack or fend off the threat

2. "Take flight": Escape, hide, retreat from, or avoid the threat

In fight-or-flight mode, our body floods with adrenaline, our heart rate increases, and our muscles tense up, ready for action. If fight mode predominates, we feel anger or rage, and the urge to attack or defend; if flight mode predominates, we feel fear or anxiety, and the urge to escape or hide.

But in a situation where it's impossible to fight off or escape from the threat—for example, when a child is being assaulted by an adult—the "freeze response" kicks in. In the grip of a full-blown freeze response, you can't move or speak, and you withdraw psychologically—your mind takes you elsewhere to escape the horror. Freeze responses are common in people with a history of trauma. So if one partner has a traumatic background—for example, if they've been abused in other relationships, either as a child or an adult—they may have a freeze response at times of conflict. They will literally freeze up, barely able to move or speak, sometimes accompanied by an "out of body" experience. This is an involuntary, automatic response, which psychologists refer to as a "dissociative state." It's nothing like the withdraw tactics mentioned earlier, and if either partner is experiencing this, it's important to seek help from a therapist with expertise in trauma.

THE CONSTRUCTIVE USE OF "TIME-OUT"

If one or both partners are so hooked that they're not able to stop their destructive tactics, it's wise to take time-out. You both go to separate rooms and take at least twenty minutes to calm down—or longer if necessary. However, for this to be a *constructive* tactic, one that's healthy for the relationship, it needs to be done in a caring, considerate way. If you storm out of the room—in silence, or with an angry diatribe—that's likely to provoke or upset your partner. To make this a constructive tactic, enhancing your relationship, both partners need to agree to four things:

1. **A caring way to suggest "time-out":** You make a pact that if either of you feels that you're getting nowhere, or things are escalating, or you're overwhelmed, or you're both hopelessly hooked and just hurting each other instead of trying to resolve things…then either one of you can suggest, in a caring way, that you both take a break. This will involve going into separate rooms and taking at least twenty minutes to unhook and reconnect with your values.

    Agree on a phrase you can use that is caring, as opposed to harsh and punitive. For example, "Can we take a break?" "I don't feel like we're getting anywhere. I'd like to call time-out," or "Can we stop this and take a breather?" If either partner finds it hard to speak at these times, agree on a nonverbal signal to use instead— like the classic "time-out" signal, where your hands form a T shape.

2. **An agreement to reconvene shortly:** Immediately after agreeing to a time-out, and before either one of you leaves, agree on when you will return. For example, "Let's come back to this in twenty minutes." Twenty minutes is the bare minimum; sometimes one or both partners may need an hour or two to effectively unhook and reconnect with their values. If it's not possible to reconvene quickly—for example, if you have to go to work—then set a time for later that day or the next day. (Best not to leave it too long, or you may forget.) Agree on the time you'll reconvene, and if it's not the same day, write it down so you remember it.

    This agreement to reconvene is essential. It prevents either partner from turning this into a destructive tactic to "detour around" the issue instead of confronting it. Alternatively, you may both prefer to agree on a "default" time-out duration, e.g., unless otherwise specified, time-out is thirty minutes.

3. **During time-out, actively unhook:** If during time-out you get trapped inside-the-mind, stewing about what your partner said or did, plunging into that psychological smog of judgment, resentment, and blame—well, there won't be any benefit. When you reconvene, you'll be just as reactive as before. So during time-out, actively use your unhooking skills. Notice and name the main stories hooking you. Practice dropping anchor, or making room, or dipping in and out of the stream.

Then reconnect with your values: What sort of partner do you want to be? What sort of relationship do you want to build? What are three values you want to embody (e.g., being kind, considerate, and fair)?

Remember, we don't challenge or dispute unhelpful thoughts in ACT; we simply unhook from them. And after we've unhooked, it's often useful to consider a different perspective: Can we look at, think about, or interpret things differently, in a way that helps us act more effectively? Ask yourself: *Is there another way to think about this, one that could help me behave more like the partner I want to be?*

To use this strategy, first connect with two or three important values. For example, do you want to be caring, fair, and considerate? If so, what's a caring, fair, and considerate way of looking at things? Perhaps something like this: *She's not always like this. She's super stressed out because of her work issues and health problems. It's understandable she's snappy and irritable. I'll try being more supportive, and see what effect that has.*

Or this: *To be fair, I've done things like this myself at times. I'm not perfect, and neither is he. A lot of the time he's quite good with this sort of thing. Maybe I can go easy on him this time.*

Or this: *They didn't do it on purpose. It was a mistake. I make mistakes too. And I guess it's not that big of a deal; it's not worth fighting over.*

You get the idea. You can't stop the judgmental thoughts and other unhelpful stories from arising, but you can unhook from them. And you can consciously connect with your values and use them to help you think about things differently, in a way that will help you behave like the person you want to be.

4. **When you reconvene, use constructive tactics:** When you reconvene, don't go back to destructive tactics. Use the new constructive ones you'll learn in the next three chapters.

If you agree in advance to these four steps—and both follow through on them—"time-out" will become a constructive, relationship-enhancing strategy. But without these steps...well, you already know how *that* goes. "Time-out" is especially useful for breaking the vicious cycle of...

Distancing and Pursuing

Attack tactics often interact with withdraw tactics to create a destructive pattern, called the "distancer/pursuer cycle." One partner (the "distancer") leaves the conflict situation because they are feeling overwhelmed. But the other partner (the "pursuer") desperately wants to resolve the conflict, so they chase after the distancer.

In these interactions, both partners are hooked by their thoughts and feelings. The distancer—hooked by intense painful emotions such as anxiety, anger, or sadness, and thoughts like "I can't handle this; I have to get out of here!"—uses withdraw tactics (refusing to talk, leaving the scene). The pursuer—also hooked by intense painful emotions, such as anxiety, anger, or sadness, and thoughts like "I have to resolve this now!"—uses attack tactics: they chase after their partner, or prevent them from leaving, or raise their voice, or criticize, judge, or threaten.

The problem is, when a distancer gets pursued, their desire to escape only gets stronger. They feel attacked, trapped, and overwhelmed, and if they can't escape, it builds and builds. Eventually, the distancer may resort to attack/defend tactics, lashing out physically or verbally. Or they may stay in withdraw mode, but instead of physically leaving, they do so mentally: they shut down, go quiet, say nothing, look away, or simply refuse to engage. (And if they have a history of trauma, they may even have a "freeze response.")

The pursuer, on the other hand, desperately wants to chase after their partner, so they can resolve the issue, settle the argument, put things to rest. At times, the main triggers for pursuit behaviors are emotions like frustration and anger, and the "I'm right, you're wrong" story. At other times, the triggers may be guilt or anxiety, especially the fear that their partner is going to abandon them. Either way, the more the distancer withdraws, the more anxious or angry (or both) the pursuer becomes. And if the pursuer stays hooked, and allows their emotions to run them, there's a rapid downhill spiral. The more intensely they pursue, the more overwhelmed their partner, and the greater their partner's motivation to distance.

So take a moment to consider these patterns of behavior. Do they ever show up in your relationship? Who tends to distance? Who tends to pursue? Do you ever swap roles?

And keep in mind, it's not that one partner is "right" and the other is "wrong." Both partners get caught in a vicious cycle; both get hurt, as does the relationship. Typically, to break these cycles, both partners need to work at it. The distancer needs to cut back on their distancing, and the pursuer needs to actively reduce their pursuit. And it's sooo much easier to make all of that happen if both agree to constructively use "time-out."

Why Do We Use Destructive Tactics?

In a difficult situation—where there's a conflict of needs, desires, interests, wishes, or goals—painful emotions and unhelpful thoughts are inevitable. And these difficult thoughts and feelings "trigger" our use of destructive tactics. When we use such tactics, they have "payoffs": they help us get what we want, or avoid what we don't want, or both.

Often these tactics work quite well, in the sense that they deliver short-term payoffs. But the problem is, none of these tactics involves any genuine consideration for our partner. Which is why, in the long term, they're destructive to the relationship.

Now let's be realistic. As I've said more than once, there's no such thing as the perfect partner. All of us, at times, use tactics from all four categories: attack, defend, detour, and withdraw. It's when these tactics are used *often* by one or both partners that significant damage occurs to the relationship. To get a better sense of this, please carefully consider these questions:

- Which of the destructive tactics do you use most often?

- When you use these methods, what effect does it have on you? (How do you feel? Are you behaving like the person you want to be?)

- When you use these methods, what effect does it have on your partner? (If you don't know, it's a good idea to ask them.)

- When you use these methods, what effect does it have on the relationship in the long term? (If you're not sure, ask your partner.)

We learn many of our destructive tactics early in life. (Most toddlers have a wealth of them.) Some of them are instinctive. Others we learn from direct experience: our parents or siblings or kids at school use these tactics on us. We may also learn some of these methods by observation: we notice the tactics that other people use on each other. And on top of all that, we may learn by trial and error: we experiment with new strategies, and if they work, we do more of them.

Take a moment to consider the most destructive of these tactics and ask yourself:

- What's the earliest you can remember using them?

- As a child, did your parents or siblings employ these tactics with you or with each other?

- Did you learn them by any other means?

If you wish to break the habit of using a particular tactic, it's often worth taking a few minutes to understand why you do it. A very quick way to do this is to "map it out" on a choice point. The easiest way to do this is to use the choice point worksheet in "Extra Bits," chapter 13. Alternatively, you can draw up your own version of the choice point: just draw two diverging arrows, and label them "toward" and "away," like the diagrams in chapter 5.

1. First, on the away arrow, describe the destructive tactic you use: What do you say and do?

2. Next, at the bottom of the diagram, write your triggers. Begin with the difficult situation: What's your partner saying or doing that's difficult for you?

3. Next, write down the thoughts and feelings that arise when you are in that situation. To help with this, remember a recent occasion when you used this tactic; recall it as vividly as you can. What was the occasion? What was your partner saying and doing? How were you feeling, or what were you thinking, just before you started to use that tactic?

4. Finally, at the top of the away arrow, write down the short-term "payoff" you get (perhaps not always, but at least sometimes) from using this tactic. Following is a list of common payoffs to help you figure this out; usually there are several for any tactic.

This tactic often helps you to:

- Escape or avoid a difficult situation (e.g., avoid something you don't want to talk about, get out of doing something you don't want to do, escape from your partner's aggressive behavior)

- Escape or avoid uncomfortable thoughts and feelings (e.g., anxiety, guilt, anger, shame, sadness)

- Gain your partner's attention, approval, or understanding

- Gain your partner's cooperation or support

- Get your needs met

- Get your own way

- Feel better (e.g., relaxed, relieved, happy)

- Feel righteous (like you are "in the right" and they are "wrong")

- Feel strong (like you stood up for yourself)

- Feel safe (like you escaped danger)

- Feel like you are working hard to address your relationship issues

There are many other possible payoffs, but most of them will fit under one or more of the categories. Occasionally, despite our best efforts, we just can't figure out what the payoffs are—and that's okay. But if we can, it's useful to have that insight.

If Your Partner Is Willing

These exercises all involve talking openly and honestly. When you are talking, make sure you do so with warmth and openness. You're talking not to score points but to deepen your bonds. And when your partner is talking, listen mindfully. Don't interrupt with smart comments. Instead, give them your full attention, with an attitude of openness and curiosity.

EXERCISE: Sharing Your Destructive Tactics

Discuss the tactics you both use in fighting. Each start by acknowledging your own tactics. Once you have listed your own, then you can invite your partner to add any others. Say something like, "Okay, I've listed every tactic I can think of that I use. Can you think of any others?" Stay open and curious, even if you don't like what your partner says. Don't get defensive: "Bullshit, I never do that!" or "I haven't done that for years." Instead try, "Wow! I don't recall doing that one," or "Ah, yes. I used to do that one a long time ago."

Next, both discuss what triggers these patterns of behavior: What situations are difficult? What thoughts and feelings hook you?

Finally, both discuss the payoffs: What do these tactics help you get or avoid? (If you're not sure, read through the list of common payoffs.)

EXERCISE: How You Learned These Tactics

Discuss how you learned these tactics. Consider the most damaging of these tactics: How far back do they go? What's the earliest you can remember using them? As a child, did your parents or siblings use these tactics with you? As a child, did you use these tactics to protect or take care of yourself?

How to Change Destructive Patterns

The choice point diagram (see chapter 5) gives us a map for changing these destructive behaviors. The first step is simply to notice you're using these tactics and acknowledge their destructiveness. The next two steps are much harder.

The second step is, when those difficult situations arise, to actively unhook yourself from all those triggering thoughts and feelings: drop anchor, make room, and so on.

The third step is, instead of continuing with your *destructive* tactic, switch over to a *constructive* tactic, like those in the next three chapters. (This may include a constructive time-out.)

And now, a reminder: it's important to look at changing your own tactics first—before you address those of your partner—because that's where you have the greatest control. And as you change your own tactics, progressively making them more constructive, you may well find your partner changes their tactics too. However, if that *doesn't* happen, you can address the issue *constructively*, by using...

CHAPTER 14

Good Communication

That's not what I said!

You're twisting my words.

That's not what I meant!

I know what you meant!

You just don't get it, do you?

I just don't know what you want.

Do you and your partner ever say things like this? I'm willing to bet you do. Why? Because you're human. And most humans are not too good at effective communication. All too often, we don't listen well to our partner, or we speak in a manner that upsets, offends, scares, or angers them. Good communication can save you a lot of hurt and arguments, resolve your problems faster, and get your needs met better. So without further ado, let's zip through the seven basic principles of good communication.

#1 Be Present

You've learned a lot about being fully present: paying attention with openness and curiosity to what is most important, here and now. This is the single most important factor in communication. If you're half-present, distracted, disengaged, on autopilot, or going through the motions, then this is what you communicate to your partner: *I'm bored. I don't care. I'm not interested. What you have to say isn't important or interesting.* Not a good start, right?

So tune in mindfully to your partner: give them your full attention, with an attitude of openness and curiosity. Listen mindfully to what they are saying; notice, with curiosity, the tone and emotion in their voice, and see whether you can detect what they're feeling.

Also, very importantly, look directly at your partner. This not only helps you to stay present, but also shows your partner that you're interested. If you look off somewhere else, it communicates the opposite. So look mindfully: notice their facial expressions and their body posture, and see whether you can gauge what they're feeling.

Stay fully present, open, and curious. And the moment you catch yourself "drifting off," unhook and refocus on your partner. (If you find this hard, it suggests the need to practice dropping anchor, chapter 7, or dipping in and out of the stream, chapter 10.)

#2 Open Up

When you're having difficult conversations, talking about your problems, grappling with your issues, raising thorny topics, asking for what you want, giving honest feedback...lots of uncomfortable feelings will arise. (Most commonly, anxiety or anger.) And as you know, our default response to such feelings is to OBEY or to STRUGGLE—neither of which is generally effective. So when difficult feelings arise, open up and make room for them. Acknowledge they're present, and allow them to be there. Let them freely come and stay and go, in their own good time. And keep your curious attention on your partner.

#3 Connect with Your Values

What sort of partner do you want to be? Caring, kind, open, understanding, considerate, honest, fair, loving, and so on? Or bitter, aggressive, scornful, cold, distant, hostile, disrespectful, contemptuous, cynical, and the like? Ask yourself, *If this exchange with my partner were taped, and posted on YouTube or TikTok, how would I like to come across? What qualities would I like viewers to see in me?*

If there's a difficult conversation to be had, it's obviously going to go better if you speak with these qualities. So be kind in the way you treat your partner; instead of harsh, judgmental, critical words, speak in a way that's kind, fair, and considerate.

When you discuss things with your partner, bring your values to the table—especially kindness, fairness, and consideration. In other words, treat your partner as a friend, not a foe. If you have these conversations with a warlike mindset—*I have to get my needs met, I have to get my own way, I have to prove I'm right, no matter what cost*—then you'll quickly go back to using destructive tactics. So go into these discussions with a caring and collaborative attitude; consider your partner's feelings and needs, as well as your own. Think "win-win": focus on making the relationship work in a way that's healthy for both of you.

#4 Adjust Your Face, Voice, and Posture

Building on the three points just discussed, consider your face, voice, and posture: Do they communicate to your partner that you're present, open, and caring? If your voice is loud or angry, if your facial expression is arrogant or contemptuous, or if your body posture is hostile (e.g., clenched fists, pointing your finger) or closed off (e.g., folded arms, looking away), then no matter how wisely you choose your words, they will not be received well. So base your face, voice, and posture on your values. Lower your voice, adopt a calm tone, take the frown off your face, drop your shoulders, open your arms, turn toward your partner, and get present.

#5 Set the Stage

If you're going to address a difficult issue, "set the stage" to make it go more smoothly. For example, pick your time wisely. When is your partner most likely to respond well? Bad times to have these discussions might be when either one of you is tired, irritable, drunk, stressed to the max, or having a shitty day. It's much better to have these discussions when you're both well and rested, both in a reasonable mood, and the environment is not too stressful (e.g., no kids running rampant in the background or disapproving in-laws within earshot).

Now it's time for a reality check. Many couples don't feel like discussing their issues when they're in a good mood. This is partly because when we're in a good mood, our problems seem smaller and easier to deal with. Also, you may think, *We're having a good day. Why spoil it?* In contrast, when we're in a bad mood, our problems seem bigger and we're more likely to be irritable or frustrated, and therefore more likely to want to talk about them. Furthermore, often arguments blow up when you aren't expecting them— so it's impossible to set the stage in advance. So while it's easy to give this advice, it's not always easy to apply it in real life.

Still, it's worth applying this principle as best you can, within the limitations of real life. It's especially helpful to give your partner advance notice: "I'd like to discuss our finances with you. Can we make time for it one night this week?" If possible, it's also helpful to step out of your usual environment: for example, discuss it during a walk in the park or over a coffee in a café.

Last but not least, connect with your values *before* you talk to your partner. Cultivate an attitude of caring, kindness, and consideration. To help with this, you may like to:

- Reflect on what your partner does that you appreciate.

- Think about your partner's strengths.

- Bring to mind a fond, loving memory that involves both of you.

- Remember, you are *both* hurting. Acknowledge your partner's pain, as well as your own. See if you can tap into some kindness and understanding, for *both* of you.

#6 First, Aim to Understand

The author Stephen Covey popularized the saying "Seek first to understand, then to be understood." This principle is essential for effective communication and negotiation. Typically, we launch into difficult conversations wanting to get our point of view across, make our needs known, and make the other person hear us and understand us. In other words, it's all about looking after ourself, trying to get our needs met; there's a lack of care and consideration for what the other party wants. And while this is normal and natural, it's not effective.

I'm sure you've experienced this many times; we all have. You're trying to get your point across, but your partner's doing the same; neither of you is mindfully listening to the other because you're so focused on what *you* want to say. You know from painful experience how ineffective this is. Often it escalates into a quarrel, or ends in a frustrating stalemate. Either way, neither party feels heard, understood, or respected.

So when you're being fully present with your partner, ramp up your curiosity to the max. Ask questions: find out how they feel, what they think, and what they want (or don't want). Pay attention with openness and curiosity and aim to get the greatest understanding possible of what's going on for your partner. Listen mindfully, and don't interrupt. (If you keep interrupting, that's a sure sign you're not mindfully listening.)

And if you're getting ready to defend yourself, or put your own viewpoint across, or state how you feel, or ask for what you want—then you're not trying hard enough to hear and understand your partner.

If you or your partner finds this difficult (as most of us do!), the practice of "reflective listening" is incredibly useful. I don't have space to cover it here, but you can read all about it in chapter 14 of "Extra Bits"—and I strongly encourage you to do so, because it's such a useful skill.

But hang on, you may be thinking, *what if I listen mindfully to what they have to say, and really make the effort to understand them, but they don't do the same for me?* Well, the good news is, after you've made a genuine effort to hear and understand your partner, they will usually be much more receptive to what you have to say. But if they don't spontaneously give you a turn to speak, or they don't listen attentively when you're speaking, then you'll need to assertively ask them to do so, as discussed in the next chapter.

#7 Choose Your Words Wisely

Harsh, critical, or judgmental words do not communicate values such as caring, loving, and kindness. So get in touch with your values and think about what you're hoping to achieve: Do you want another quarrel, or do you want a better relationship? If the latter, then what sort of words would be most effective? If you were addressing this issue with your best friend or someone you highly admire, what would you say to that person? How would you phrase it?

There's a good reason why I left this principle to last. You see, the words you choose are the frosting on the cake, and the first six principles are the cake beneath that frosting. If you don't have principles 1 to 6 in place, you'll either be unable to choose your words wisely (because you're hooked and reactive) or you'll find they fall on deaf ears. In the next chapter, we'll cover several ways to choose words wisely—but the other principles need to come first.

Easy to Read, Not So Easy to Do

So the seven principles of effective communication are:

1. Be present

2. Open up

3. Connect with your values

4. Adjust your face, voice, and posture

5. Set the stage

6. First, aim to understand

7. Choose your words wisely

Now, it's important to be realistic. While it's easy to read about this stuff, it's not so easy to do in real life. New skills take time, effort, and lots and lots of practice to develop. And relationships don't improve suddenly and dramatically; patience and persistence are required. But as the old saying goes, "The journey of a thousand miles begins with one step." And small changes, over time, can have dramatic effects.

So look for opportunities to apply any of these seven principles, in any way you can, no matter how small a gesture it may be. Even if you can be just a little more present or open to your feelings or connected with your values; just a little more warm and open in your face, voice, and body posture; just a little more keen on understanding your partner; just a little more careful with your words; or just slightly better at picking the time and place to have difficult conversations. Any one of those changes is a step in the right direction.

CHAPTER 15

The Power of Assertiveness

Have you ever hung out with a puppy dog? If so, you know it only cares about one thing: *you!* The moment you come through the door, it's ecstatic to see you: jumping up, wagging its tail, trying to lick you. It never gets bored with you and never turns nasty. And it's always so disappointed when you have to leave. You could ignore it, shout at it, mistreat it—and still it would just want to be with you, to "love you" and please you. A puppy dog pays no attention to its own needs; it's all about giving!

Have you ever hung out with a shark? No, me neither. But you've seen them on TV, and you know what they're like. The shark doesn't care about you one bit. It's only interested in its own needs—namely food. If you feed it well, it probably won't attack you. But if you don't feed it, you're breakfast. Try to bond with a shark and you're wasting your time.

In a healthy human relationship, we need to find a balance between these two extremes. If the relationship is all about you—your needs, your wants, your desires—your partner will see you as a shark: they're always providing food to stop you from eating them, but getting nothing back from you in return. This may work for you, but it's not good for your partner's health and well-being. On the other hand, if your relationship is all about pleasing your partner, and you constantly neglect your own needs, then you'll start to feel like a helpless, neglected puppy dog.*

---

*   Many thanks to Tony Wallace, a counselor in Canberra, for this metaphor.

It's rare that one partner is all shark and the other is all puppy dog; we've all got aspects of both these creatures inside us. But most of us would benefit from finding a better balance: to become a compassionate, caring human being who is respectful of *both* our own needs *and* those of our partner.

Are there areas of your relationship where you are perhaps a bit too shark-like? Although you may get your needs met in the short term, what long-term effects does this have on your partner and your relationship? To step out of shark mode, you need to tune in to your values around caring, consideration, kindness, and fairness, and remind yourself of your partner's rights. That doesn't mean turning into a puppy dog. It simply means that you actively invest in your partner's health, growth, and well-being as well as your own.

Now, in what areas of your relationship do you tend to take the role of the puppy dog? And what is this costing you in the long run? The puppy-dog role may give you some short-term benefits. It may help you avoid fears of rejection, abandonment, or being hurt. It may help you avoid anxiety around conflict. It may even make you feel good about yourself, because you're living your values of being caring, loving, and supportive. But it costs you heavily in terms of health and vitality. In the long term, it leads you to feel burned-out, downtrodden, resentful, or drained. To step out of puppy-dog mode, you need to tune into values like self-respect, self-nurture, and self-care, and remind yourself of your own rights. That doesn't mean turning into a shark. It simply means you look after your own health and well-being as well as investing in that of your partner.

To find a good balance between meeting our own needs *and* those of our partner, in ways that enable the relationship to thrive, we will need to use…

Assertiveness Skills

To understand the concept of assertiveness, it's best to contrast it with passivity and aggression. "Passivity" (or "passive behavior") means putting the needs of others ahead of your own, at significant cost to your own health and well-being. When you're being passive (like the puppy dog), you neglect your own needs, and instead of standing up for yourself, you allow others to "walk all over you." "Aggression" (or "aggressive behavior") means standing up for yourself and taking care of your needs in a way that's disrespectful and uncaring of others. When you're being aggressive (like the shark), you don't care about the feelings, rights, or needs of the other party; it's all about getting your own way.

"Assertiveness" (or "assertive behavior") is radically different to both passivity and aggression. It means standing up for yourself and taking care of your needs in a way that is fair and considerate of *both yourself and others*. When being assertive, you respect your own rights, while also respecting the rights of your partner. So it's very important to…

Know Your Bill of Rights

Back in chapter 2, I shared a basic bill of rights for any relationship. Here it is again. (There's a copy in "Extra Bits.") Please read it carefully and notice your reactions. At the bottom, there are three incomplete statements; please complete them by writing in (or imagining) any other rights you consider important.

- I have the right to be treated fairly and considerately.

- I have the right to make my needs equally important to those of others.

- I have the right to decline requests, provided I do so in a way that is fair and considerate.

- I have the right to be fallible, imperfect, and make mistakes.

- I have the right to ask for what I want, provided I do so in a way that is fair and considerate.

- I have the right to feel the way I feel.

- I have the right to honestly state my thoughts, feelings, ideas, and opinions, provided I do so in a way that is fair and considerate.

- I have the right to stand up for my rights, provided I do so fairly, with consideration of the rights of others.

- I have the right to _____

- I have the right to _____

- I have the right to _____

You'll notice that many of these rights contain a clause: *provided I do so in a way that is fair and considerate.* The proviso is there to encourage assertiveness rather than aggression. If you stand up for your rights in a way that's unfair or inconsiderate, then you'll be acting aggressively, not assertively.

Remember, your partner has the same rights as you—including *the right to be treated fairly and considerately.* If you don't respect that right, if you trample over it to get your own way, that's aggression—and it's toxic to your partner's health and well-being. In chapter 13, we looked at destructive tactics we all use at times to get our needs met. All of our "attack" and "defend" tactics are aggressive. And many (but not all) of our "detour" and "withdraw" tactics are technically classed as "passive-aggressive," because they involve concealed or indirect aggression; they allow you to express your anger, frustration, or resentment without directly stating how you feel. All these destructive tactics share one thing in common: they all lack respect for the rights of the other party—especially their right to be treated fairly and considerately. We all use some of these tactics some of the time, and that need not be a major problem, but the more often they're used, the more destructive they are to the relationship.

On the flip side, if you don't respect your own rights, rarely stand up for yourself, or frequently neglect your own needs, then that's toxic to your own health and well-being. So assertiveness involves a healthy balance of self-care and caring for your partner, standing up for your own rights while also respecting theirs.

Assertiveness skills fall into two main categories:

1. **Making requests:** asking for what you want, in a fair and considerate manner

2. **Declining requests:** saying no to what you don't want, in a fair and considerate manner

Let's start with...

How to Ask for What You Want

Often asking for what you want doesn't require assertiveness; it's just a matter of "asking nicely." And by that, I don't mean begging or pleading; I simply mean asking politely. You have a right to ask for what you want; and your partner has a right to be spoken to politely. So make your request a friendly one: without snapping, or criticizing, or demands, threats, or insults. Many people find this hard to do because they won't let go of stories such as these:

"I shouldn't have to ask. They should just do it."

"I've tried asking nicely. She never listens."

"Why should I have to ask nicely? He doesn't deserve it."

"If I ask nicely, they'll ignore me. They only ever agree when I get angry."

Are you willing to unhook from these stories? These thoughts may be partly true—or even totally true—but how does it work for your relationship if you hold on to them tightly?

Regardless of what has happened in the past, the fact remains: one of the simplest ways to get your needs met *and* also build a healthy relationship is just to ask nicely. Instead of "Do this," "Get that," "Have you done XYZ yet?" "Can I have...," use words like "please" or "Is it okay with you?" or

"Would you mind?" For example: "Please can you get me a beer from the fridge?" "Would you mind taking the trash out, please?" "Is it okay with you if I take the car tonight?"

There are many other ways to do this. For example, if you're asking for something that your partner is often hesitant or reluctant to do, you could start off with a compliment, an expression of appreciation, or both: "Honey, I really appreciate the efforts you've been making to tidy up after yourself. I know it doesn't come naturally to you, but it makes my life so much easier." Next, when you make your request, you can use phrases such as "I'd be very grateful if..." or "I'd like it if..." or "I'd really appreciate it if..." or "It would mean a lot to me if..."

Notice this involves the principles of positive reinforcement, which we covered in chapter 12: catch them doing it right, carrot versus stick. Also notice what your mind has to say about this idea; at first, it may be quite reluctant. For example, here's how Sarah reacted when I suggested this:

Sarah:	But I'd be lying. I don't feel grateful if Steve puts the kids to bed. He's just doing what he ought to do. Why should I be grateful for that?
Russ:	It sounds like you're a bit hooked.
Sarah:	By what?
Russ:	By the "Steve should do what I want" story.
Sarah:	*(aghast)* Are you saying he should be allowed to do what he wants? Have a beer, sit in front of the TV, and leave it all up to me?
Russ:	Not at all. That's the passive option, and it's not healthy. What I'm saying is, if you want Steve to put the kids to bed *and* you also want to build a better relationship, then what's going to work best—showing gratitude when he does what you want, and asking him nicely to do more of it, or taking the aggressive attitude of "About time you pulled your weight, Mister!"?

Sarah: But I shouldn't have to ask him. He should just do it.

Russ: Sarah, there are millions of people on this planet who
            would totally agree with you. This is not a question of
            right or wrong, true or false. It's a question of what
            works best for you and your relationship in the long
            term. If you hold that "should" story too tightly, and
            allow it to dictate the way you talk to Steve, will it
            make your relationship better or worse?

Sarah: (reluctantly, sighing) Worse.

It's very hard to unhook from our "shoulds," but we need to hold them
lightly if we want our relationship to thrive. So notice and name these
stories when they show up, and let them come and go. Then drop anchor,
get present, and bring in your new assertiveness skills.

Assertiveness is a huge topic, and in this chapter we're going to focus
mainly on assertive *language*: how you can phrase things to get the best
results. But before we get into that, a reminder: in these interactions,
words are the "frosting on the cake." If you want your words to land well
and have a positive effect, you'll need to apply the principles of effective
communication:

1. **Be present.** You'll need to be fully present and focused on your
    partner.

2. **Open up.** You'll need to drop anchor and make room for all those
    difficult feelings that arise.

3. **Connect with your values.** You'll need to be in touch with your
    values of caring, kindness, and consideration, keeping in mind that
    you want the relationship to thrive.

4. **Adjust your face, voice, and posture.** If you look bored or threat-
    ening, or your voice is laden with scorn, or you're pointing your
    finger or folding your arms across your chest, or you're not actually

looking at your partner, that will undermine any words you say, no matter how carefully chosen they are. So lower your voice, soften your face, adopt an open posture, and look directly at your partner.

If these four fundamentals aren't in place, your words will not have the desired effect. In some, but not all cases, principles 5 and 6 also apply:

5. **Set the stage.** If possible, pick a time and place conducive to a positive exchange. It isn't always possible to do this, but whenever you can, it helps.

6. **First, aim to understand.** If it's a longer conversation and your partner wants to share their feelings, opinions, or needs, or if the discussion becomes a negotiation, bring openness and curiosity to the exchange. Listen mindfully, be present, and make the effort to genuinely understand what's going on for your partner, *before* you share your side of things.

And then there's principle 7, the frosting on the cake:

7. **Choose your words wisely.** With principles 1 through 4 in place (and, if relevant, 5 and 6), we can bring in the final principle. And that's what the rest of this chapter is largely about. So let's kick off with a look at…

"I" Statements

The most basic form of assertiveness is a simple statement that clearly expresses our needs, feelings, or opinions using the term "I." For example:

"I need to leave in half an hour."

"I feel really happy that you managed to sort that out."

"I enjoyed the movie, but the ending was a bit disappointing."

You can readily use these statements to praise, compliment, share information, or raise an issue:

"I wasn't expecting you to say that. I'll need to think about it. I'll get back to you shortly."

"I really appreciate what you did."

Disclosing Feelings

You can use "I" statements to simply share your feelings:

"I feel awkward."

"I'm stressed."

"I'm feeling anxious about this."

When we use "I" statements to express our feelings this way, not only does it help us unhook a little, but it also communicates to others that we're taking responsibility for our own feelings. This is very different from "you" statements, such as "You make me so angry," which indicate we are blaming others for the way we feel.

Basic Requests

Simple "I" statements are very useful for making straightforward requests. And adding the word "please" often lends impact. For example, notice the aggressive quality of this "you" statement: "You've had your say, now it's my turn!" Compare that with this assertive "I" statement: "I'd like a chance to speak, please. Can I tell you my side of things?"

Following are some more examples. In the previous chapter, we discussed the principle: *first, aim to understand.* I mentioned that if you try this, but your partner doesn't reciprocate, you can assertively ask them to do so. These examples will give you some ideas for how to do this.

Aggressive "You" Statement	Assertive "I" Statement
"Will you stop butting in?!"	"Please stop interrupting me. I allowed you to talk freely; please do the same for me."
"You are so rude!"	"I don't like it when you call me names. Can you please let me speak without doing that?"
"Will you shut up for a moment and let me speak?!"	"I would like a chance to talk about my side of things. Can you please let me speak, and listen carefully, in the same way that I just did for you?"
"Why don't you ever wash the dog?!"	"I notice that, for the last few months, I'm usually the one washing the dog."

Raising Issues and Sharing Feelings

Most of us are quick to point the finger at our partner, to accuse or blame them for what they've said or done. This usually leads to an unproductive quarrel. But if we raise issues in a fair and considerate manner, and disclose our feelings without any blame, it will usually have a positive impact. Here are some examples:

"You" Statements: Judging, Blaming, or Accusing	"I" Statements: Stating How You Feel Without Blaming or Accusing
"Why are you always so messy?"	"I feel frustrated when I get home after work and the house is a mess."
"You never listen to me. You always go and do what you want to do."	"I feel frustrated when my wishes aren't taken into account."
"You said you were going to call me, but you didn't!"	"When I didn't hear from you, I was really worried."

"You" Statements: Judging, Blaming, or Accusing	"I" Statements: Stating How You Feel Without Blaming or Accusing
"You're always shouting at me!"	"When you shout at me, I get a sick feeling in my stomach, and I feel like I want to run away."
"You make me so angry!"	"I feel angry when you do things like that."
"You make me feel useless!"	"When you say things like that to me, I feel sad, and my mind tells me I'm useless."

Leading with a "you" statement will make your partner feel accused or blamed and will likely provoke an argument. Leading with an "I" statement is much less confrontational and paves the way for a constructive discussion. (But watch out for sneaky "I" statements that are really aggressive "you" statements in disguise. For example: *I feel like you're not pulling your weight. I feel like you leave all the chores to me. I think you're being lazy.*)

"Video Descriptions"

Suppose we want our partner to start or stop doing something, and basic assertive requests (like those described) aren't working. If so, we can make an assertive request more impactful by adding a "video description." This is a factual description of the relevant behavior, without any judgment: it's what a video camera would record, as opposed to how a person would judge it. For example, in the top row of the previous table, both statements are judgments, not factual descriptions: *you're always so messy; the house is a mess.* However, the second statement is better than the first. Why? Because the first one is a personal attack: *you are messy.* A personal attack includes any statement to the effect of "you are X," where X is a harsh global judgment: *you are lazy, selfish, arrogant,* etc. This is always an aggressive stance: an attack or a defend tactic. The second statement—*the house is a mess*—is better because it's not a personal attack; it's not a global judgment about the whole person. However, it's still a judgmental description rather than a factual one. In contrast, here's a nonjudgmental video description: *there are dirty dishes and food spills on the table.*

A nonjudgmental, factual description like this is much more effective than a judgmental one for two good reasons. One: it's likely to be perceived as a fairer, more accurate account (as opposed to unfair or inaccurate). Two: it's therefore much less likely to be contested. If you say, *there's mess everywhere*, or *you're always messy*, or *the house is a pigsty*, your partner may well fire back with *that's not true*, or *that's not fair*, or *you're exaggerating.* You then both start arguing over the words you've used, rather than dealing with the real issue.

Note that video descriptions don't include words like "always" or "never"; those terms are exaggerations and almost always trigger a defensive response: "I don't *always* do that!" "Oh yeah? If I *never* do that, then how come just yesterday I did ABC?" (In the left-hand column of the previous table, you can see four examples of "always" or "never" accusations.)

"I" statements are much better than "you" statements. However, to get the best results—that is, a partner willing to listen to negative feedback, and actually take it on board—we need to include video descriptions. Following are some examples. In the first column, there are "you" statements with judgmental descriptions; in the second column, there are "I" statements with judgmental descriptions; and in the third column, there are "I" statements with video descriptions.

"You" Statement with Judgmental Description	"I" Statement with Judgmental Description	"I" Statement with Video Description
"You're always nagging me."	"I feel irritated when you keep nagging me."	"I feel irritated when you ask me to do something four or five times in a short space of time."
"You're so lazy."	"I feel quite annoyed when you're being lazy."	"I feel quite annoyed when you say you're going to take the trash out later, but then you don't do it."

"You" Statement with Judgmental Description	"I" Statement with Judgmental Description	"I" Statement with Video Description
"You're so unreliable."	"I feel disappointed when you're unreliable."	"I felt really disappointed last night; you said you were going to be home by 10:00 p.m., but you didn't get back until 1:00 a.m. and you didn't call to let me know."

If you think this all sounds very convoluted, rest assured: it's not necessary to speak this way all the time. These phrases are best used for tricky, sticky situations, when your partner isn't hearing you. Most of the time, we can use shorter, simpler expressions, like the basic assertive requests we covered first: "I don't like it when you speak to me that way," or "Please don't talk to me like that; I don't like it."

The "P" Word

Sorry to mention the "p" word yet again, but if you want to get the hang of these new ways of speaking, practice is absolutely essential, especially when it comes to the more challenging methods we cover next. So I strongly recommend that you practice in front of a mirror—or better still, record yourself on a camera. As you rehearse these statements, work on your face, voice, and posture to convey a sense of calmness and openness. Without such rehearsal, you will either forget to use these new skills or you'll try to use them and screw it up. However, a little bit of practice goes a loooong way, and in "Extra Bits" you'll find a number of simple exercises you can do on a regular basis to build these skills.

If your partner is supportive, let them know what you're doing; explain that you're practicing new ways of communicating, in the hope this will help your relationship. (If your partner's willing to read this chapter, so much the better.) Let them know you may sound a bit awkward or clumsy at first, because you're experimenting with new ways of speaking, and ask for their support and encouragement. This isn't essential, but it helps if you can get it. And it's hugely helpful if they're willing to try this way of speaking, too. (If your partner's not interested or supportive, that's disappointing; make room for your painful feelings and practice lots of self-compassion. And don't let that stop you from learning and applying these new skills.)

Three-Part Assertive Statements

When it comes to getting your needs met, three-part assertive statements do the heavy lifting. The basic formula is this:

I feel X when you do Y, and I'd prefer it if you could do Z.

For example, *I feel frustrated when I get home after work and there are dirty dishes and food spills on the table,* and *I'd really appreciate it if you could wipe the table clean and put the dishes in the dishwasher.*

What you're doing here is an "I" statement first (expressing your feelings), followed by a video description of your partner's behavior, and ending with a request for a new behavior you'd like them to do instead.

And you can change this order if preferred: *When you do Y, I feel X, and I'd prefer it if you could do Z.* For example: *When you ask me to do something four or five times in a short space of time, I feel really irritated. Can you please just ask me once, and trust me to do it?*

When you're making the request at the end, it needs to be specific, as illustrated in the previous examples. If your request is vague, it could be misinterpreted. Consider the first example; suppose the request was this: *I'd really appreciate it if you could tidy up.* Now what does that actually mean? Your idea of "tidying up" may be very different than your partner's. For them, "tidying up" might just mean wiping up the food spills. For you, it means doing that *and* putting the dishes in the dishwasher. So without being clear and specific about what you're asking, you're setting the stage for a future argument about whether or not your partner did what you requested. To help with this, it's useful to revisit the idea of a video description: What does "tidying up" look like on a video? It looks like *wiping the table and putting the dishes in the dishwasher.* So *that's* what you ask for.

And remember that you're *requesting*, not commanding. So we're back to that idea of "asking nicely." Useful phrases for asking include: *I'd prefer it, I'd appreciate it, I'd be grateful, I'd like it, it would mean a lot to me, it'd be so helpful.*

The more assertive you are in your requests—the more fair and considerate, and the less judgmental and aggressive—the more likely your partner is to respond positively. Obviously, this won't always happen. Remember, this a way to *influence* others; it's not a way to *control* them. Assertiveness increases the *probability* that your partner will behave more like you want, but there are no guarantees. So what can we do…

When Things Go Awry

Sometimes your assertive request will trigger a negative response from your partner, and they'll resort to destructive tactics: attack, defend, detour, or withdraw. For example, in attack mode, they may mock or try to ridicule you. In defend mode, they may call you a hypocrite and point out all the times when you do similar things to those you're complaining about. In detour mode, they may agree to your request but not follow through on it. In withdraw mode, they may refuse to discuss it and leave the room.

When your partner resorts to destructive tactics, you'll have a strong desire to respond in kind: you'll feel the pull either to be aggressive or to just passively give up. In these moments, your unhooking skills are essential. An emotional storm will blow up, and you'll need to drop anchor. The next step is to see whether you can de-escalate the situation by saying something like: "I'm not trying to attack, or judge, or blame you. I've no desire to do anything like that. I love you, and I want us to have a better relationship."

And then you'll need to ramp up your assertiveness and take it to the next level. There are six powerful assertiveness techniques for effectively responding to any barrier, but unfortunately, there's not enough room here to cover them. However, I've described them in chapter 15 of "Extra Bits," along with tips for giving and receiving negative feedback. I strongly encourage you download this extra material and read it thoroughly, so you're prepared if things don't go as planned.

How to Keep Changes Going

What if your partner agrees to your request and does their new behavior for a while, but then it starts to drop off, and they slide back into their old patterns? The best way to prevent this is positive reinforcement: "catch them doing it right" and "carrot versus stick." Actively notice and appreciate the changes they've made and express your gratitude. And not just once or twice, but ongoing. In other words, if you want the new behavior to persist, don't take it for granted. Comment on it often; let your partner know that you appreciate it. Thank them. Tell them what it means to you. And do so often. (And if your mind says, *I shouldn't have to*—you know what to do.) If, despite all that, they do backslide, then again make an assertive request, but preface it with appreciation: *I really appreciated it when you started doing XYZ; it made a big difference to me. And I've noticed you're not doing it so much now, and at times you're even back to doing ABC. It would be a huge help if you could go back to doing more XYZ.*

Overcoming Your Own Barriers

Many people don't practice assertiveness because of their own psychological barriers. They get hooked by feelings of fear and anxiety and thoughts such as: "I'm not good enough," "My needs don't matter," "I'm not important," "If I'm assertive, my partner won't like it; they'll resent, attack, or reject me," "It's too hard," "It's too scary," and so on. If thoughts and feelings like this are arising for you, recognize that's normal—but don't let it stop you. Practice your unhooking skills. Notice and name those stories; open up and make room for feelings of fear and anxiety. Do the more challenging mindfulness exercises to build your psychological muscles. For your thoughts, practice dipping in and out of the stream, listening in to your mind, and visualizing leaves on a stream (see chapter 9). And for your feelings, practice TAME (see chapter 10). Most important of all, practice lots of self-compassion, including kind self-talk and the "kind hand" exercise (also in chapter 10).

Over time, this will take the impact out of those self-judgmental thoughts and scary feelings; they'll still show up, but you won't need to let them hold you back. You can then connect with your values, remember why you're learning these new skills, and ask yourself this question: *In the service of building the relationship I want, am I willing to make room for these difficult thoughts and feelings?*

Declining Requests and Setting Boundaries

Relationships involve give-and-take and compromise. Your partner won't always agree to your requests, and you won't always agree to theirs. And both of you have the right to decline requests, as long as you do so fairly and considerately. In other words, the way we decline requests is just as important as the way we make them.

Some of us find it hard to say "no" when others make requests, especially if the person requesting is pushy or demanding or giving us a "guilt trip." Others find it easy to say "no," but they tend to do so in a forceful or inconsiderate manner, which is most unpleasant for the person who made the request. So it's worth learning how to decline requests assertively—in a fair and considerate way that's healthy for the relationship.

Declining requests is important for your own health and well-being, especially if others are trying to manipulate, coerce, or take advantage. It's also very useful when you've got so many things on your plate that agreeing to another will overwhelm you.

To decline a request assertively, be direct, firm, and honest, while also being fair and considerate. And remember: this is one of your personal rights, so you don't need to apologize for saying "no." For example, you may say: "I'd like to help, but I can't." or "Thanks for the offer, but I'm going to say no; that's not really my thing." Or "Thanks for thinking of me, but I'm going to pass." You don't have to give a reason for saying no, but it is often helpful to do so: "I'm so busy," "I'm too tired," "I've got so many things on my plate," "I just don't like that sort of thing."

If you're not sure what the request actually involves, ask for more information, including specific details, such as when, where, what, with whom, and for how long. And if you feel like you want time to consider it, then postpone giving your answer: "I need a bit of time to think about it. I'll get back to you shortly." "I'm not sure. Let me think on it for a while." And if you can think of alternatives that might help the person requesting meet their needs, it's often helpful to suggest them: "Maybe you could try XYZ instead?"

Another important aspect of assertiveness is setting "healthy boundaries." These are limits or "borders" you place on how you spend your time and energy, what you do with your body, and how you allow others to treat you. When you establish clear boundaries, it keeps you safe, protects your health and well-being, and prevents others from manipulating or taking advantage of you. Setting healthy boundaries in a way that's conducive to a good relationship usually requires both making requests assertively *and* declining requests assertively. Here are a few examples:

Time boundary: "I'm happy to keep watching this show for another half hour, but then I'm going to bed."

Space boundary: "Please leave me alone; I have to get this task completed for work."

Social boundary: "I can't go to the movies with you on Saturday. I've arranged to go out with my friends."

Physical boundary: "Please don't touch me like that. I don't like it."

Conversational boundary: "I'd prefer not to talk about this right now. I'm tired, and I just want to chill. Can we talk about this tomorrow, after dinner?"

Mental boundary: "Clearly, we have very different opinions about this. And your opinion is valid, but please don't try to force it on me. Let's agree to differ."

There's a whole lot more to these topics, including how to handle someone who "won't take no for an answer." So once again, I strongly encourage you to read the additional materials included in chapter 15 of "Extra Bits." That knowledge will serve you well when it comes to...

CHAPTER 16

The Art of Negotiation

What is it you want most from your partner? Affection, understanding, inti-macy, respect, approval? More sex, more support, more help, more social life, more family time? To reach some agreement on buying a car, or having a child, or moving to a new home?

Whatever you want, here's a fact: either you will get it or you won't. (I can 100 percent guarantee this—or your money back!) For as the famous guru Mick Jagger wisely said, "You can't always get what you want." However, the *likelihood* of you getting it is greater if you drop the destructive tactics and instead rely on...

Fair and Considerate Negotiation

There are those two words again: fair and considerate. Without fairness, without consideration for both partners' rights, needs, and feelings, negotia-tion rapidly devolves into a maelstrom of destructive tactics: fight, defend, detour, withdraw. Luckily, you already know a lot about fair, considerate negotiation. It involves all seven principles of communication. You need to be present, open, and in touch with your values; adjust your face, voice, and posture to reflect a friendly attitude; set the stage (if possible); aim to under-stand (before aiming to be understood); and choose your words wisely, assertively requesting what you want.

The fifth principle, setting the stage, can make a huge difference. Instead of catching your partner by surprise, you could say, "There's an issue I really would like to talk to you about." You then suggest a time to discuss it: "Could we please discuss it tonight, after dinner?" Ask if they want to know what it's about, and if they say yes, summarize it in one or two sentences using nonjudgmental, nonblaming language.

Sometimes they may want to talk about it immediately, or they may use a destructive tactic: *Not that again! Can't you just give me a break?!* If so, pause, drop anchor, get present, and be assertive: "I'm not ready to discuss this right now. Can we please agree to discuss this at [specific time]?" Agreeing to a specific time is very important; if you just vaguely agree to discuss it "later," there's a good chance it will never happen.

Another important part of setting the stage is to consider, in advance, the outcomes you're hoping for. There are three questions to consider:

1. What do I want for myself?

2. What do I want for my partner?

3. What do I want for the relationship?

Question 1 comes naturally to us, but questions 2 and 3 often don't. If you consider all three questions in advance, that will help shift you out of "shark mode" and into a more caring, considerate mindset.

The sixth principle—first, aim to understand—is often the hardest to apply. We're so keen to get our needs met that it's difficult to put that aside and really hear what our partner has to say. But if we make the effort to genuinely understand our partner's perspective—what they want, what they're feeling, how they see things—the payoffs are often huge. When your partner feels heard and understood, they're much more likely to listen to your side of things, which paves the way for effective negotiation. (Once again, I encourage you to read about "reflective listening," in chapter 14 of "Extra Bits"; it will help you enormously with this principle.)

The seventh principle—choose your words wisely—and the fourth principle—adjust your face, voice, and posture—are both extremely important. Let's return again to John Gottman (Gottman and Silver 1999): his research shows that many discussions go badly right from the outset because of a "harsh start-up." If you kick off with judgmental, accusatory language, or a loud, angry voice, you're very likely to trigger a quarrel. So quiet your voice, speak calmly, adopt an open posture, and choose caring, considerate words, including "I" statements and video descriptions.

It's often useful to begin with a statement of genuine appreciation, for example: "I really appreciate the effort you've been making to…" or "I love you very much, and I've noticed you've been doing XYZ, and that means a lot to me." And then follow this with an expression of intent: "I want to talk about this because it's important to me, and it's impacting our relationship, and I want things to be better between us." (Obviously, convert this into your own way of speaking, so it comes more naturally to you.)

Then explain (nonjudgmentally) what's bothering you, and why, and how you feel about it, and ask (nicely) for what you want. Hopefully, your partner will respond positively and you'll then discuss what they want, and what you want, and come to an agreement.

In an ideal world, both you and your partner will use the seven principles, but obviously that's not realistic for everyone. Still, even if you are the only one using these principles, things are likely to work out better than if you fall back on those old destructive tactics.

Three Types of Outcome

There are three types of outcome from these negotiations: win-win, win-lose, and lose-lose. Win-win outcomes are the best: both partners get their needs met in ways that are healthy for the relationship. A lose-lose outcome means neither partner gets what they want, and both are unhappy about it. And a win-lose outcome means one partner gets what they want to the detriment of the other. Both win-lose and lose-lose outcomes are destructive to the relationship.

Strategies for Healthy Outcomes

The five most popular strategies for achieving win-win outcomes are 1) put aside goals and focus on needs, 2) tit for tat, 3) willing sacrifice, 4) sharing the load, and 5) willing compromise. Let's look at each one.

1. **Put aside goals and focus on needs:** Louise and Jennifer both enjoy going to parties. However, Louise likes to get to bed before midnight, whereas Jennifer likes to party on for hours. They've had lots of arguments over their differing goals: Louise's goal to leave before midnight, and Jennifer's goal to stay on until at least 2 or 3 a.m. So in this strategy, you put aside the goals you disagree on and instead look at ways to meet your underlying needs.

   Louise needs a good night's sleep so she can function well the next day. Jennifer needs freedom, so she can choose for herself how long she will party on. Therefore, instead of fighting over what time to leave the party, they agree to this: When Louise is tired and ready to go, she will go home by herself in good grace, and will not try to persuade Jennifer to go with her. And Jennifer will caringly escort Louise to the car or taxi, and will not attempt to dissuade her from leaving.

2. **Tit for tat:** As the name suggests, this strategy is a simple trade-off: you do this for me, and I'll do that for you. For example, this time around, Louise agrees to stay up and party late; but at the next party, they'll both leave together and get home before midnight. In other words, on a given occasion one partner's needs get priority; in exchange, on another occasion, the other partner's needs will get priority. Thus, over time, both partners' needs get equally met. A variant on this is "taking turns": "This time, I'll chose the movie we see; next time, you choose." "This time we'll go to my parents' house on Christmas day; next time, yours."

3. **Willing sacrifice:** One of Liam's good friends is getting married. But Victor's high school reunion is taking place on the very same day. Victor really wants to go to his reunion, but he chooses to willingly forego it, as a gesture of love and caring for Liam. Victor does

this wholeheartedly, without any resentment, in line with his values of being loving, caring, and supportive. It's a win for Liam: he gets what he wants. It's also a win for Victor: he has the satisfaction of giving a genuine gift from the heart, and building a lot of goodwill in the process.

4. **Sharing the load:** This strategy works well with tasks that neither partner relishes; basically, you share the load between you. "You cook dinner, and I'll wash up afterward." "You buy the groceries, and I'll unpack the bags and put the groceries away." "You drop the kids off, and I'll pick them up."

5. **Willing compromise:** The gist of this strategy is, "I'll meet you halfway." Louise wants to leave the party at 11:30 p.m. Jennifer wants to leave at 1:30 a.m. They agree to leave at 12:30 a.m. Neither gets exactly what they want, but they both partially get their needs met. This is the most common resolution for the almost universal issue of housework. Victor likes to keep the house spotlessly clean and tidy. Liam doesn't have the same standards; he rarely notices "mess" and isn't much bothered by it. However, knowing how much it means to Victor, Liam agrees to up his game: he commits to a number of activities to keep the house clean and tidy: putting his shoes away, hanging up his coat, stacking dirty dishes in the dishwasher, and so on. Victor, on the other hand, knows that Liam will never be as clean and tidy as he is, so he lowers his expectations, unhooks from his "shoulds," and actively appreciates the efforts Liam is making. Compromise works reasonably well, provided both partners agree to it *willingly*. If either partner is grudging or resentful, it doesn't work well at all. To clarify this, let's briefly discuss...

The Importance of Willingness

For any of these five strategies to be truly win-win, they need to be done *willingly*. If either partner does any of these things grudgingly or resentfully (hooked by *I shouldn't have to* or *it's not fair*), out of a sense of hopelessness, or because they are scared of what will happen if they don't, well, then it's not an act of *willingness*. And that means it's not a win-win. When one partner is unwilling, it's a win-lose; when both are unwilling, it's a lose-lose. Both win-lose and lose-lose outcomes damage the relationship.

Needs Versus Goals

Let's now revisit the first of the strategies: *put aside goals, focus on needs*. This bears exploring in more detail. Let's use the example of Antonio and Maria, a couple in their late fifties, married with three adult children. Maria wanted sex at least once a week, but Antonio preferred once a month. Maria had tried criticizing him, pleading with him, insulting him, dressing up sexily, demanding sex, reminding him of his "duties as a man," comparing him to her friends' husbands, telling him she feels unloved, asking him to make her "feel like a real woman," and so on. She'd been doing this for years, but the more pressure Maria applied, the less Antonio's interest in sex.

How did they break this vicious cycle? Well, I asked them both to put aside their goals and instead look at their underlying needs.

Maria's needs were sensuality, connection, physical intimacy, affection, love, having fun, and enjoyment. Antonio's needs were much the same as Maria's: affection, sensuality, physical intimacy, and having fun. But in addition, he identified needs for autonomy and freedom: to be free to choose for himself how often he has sex, without being pressured or manipulated into it.

After you identify needs, the next step is to brainstorm different ways of meeting them. When brainstorming, you come up with as many ideas as possible, and you don't discard any of them—even if your mind says they're "silly," "bad," or "won't work." You don't get attached to any of them, either. You're simply generating ideas—not judging them as good, bad, right, or wrong. Here's what came out of Maria's and Antonio's brainstorm: To meet their needs for physical intimacy, love, affection, and connection, they could hold hands, cuddle, hug, massage, have heart-to-heart conversations, go out for romantic dinners—and yes, also have sex. With regard to having fun and enjoyment, there were already many ways they did that, from going to the movies to walking on the beach. In other words, there were many ways that both Maria and Antonio could meet their needs, regardless of how often they had sex.

Now as it happened, once Maria dropped the goal for weekly intercourse, things improved dramatically. With the pressure off, Antonio became more physically intimate. As long as Maria didn't pressure him to have intercourse, he was happy to do a whole lot more *sensual* but not *sexual* activities, such as hugging, cuddling, and kissing. Maria was pleasantly surprised to find that they could connect just as deeply through cuddling, kissing, and talking as they could through having sex. They also made a deal that if Maria became highly aroused, she would masturbate rather than pressuring Antonio for sex. (And they both had to unhook from some very unhelpful stories around that!)

So, Maria let go of her specific goal (for weekly sex), but found many other ways to get her needs met. And throughout it all she lived her core values: being loving, caring, open, present, and flexible. Just about everything she said and did to get her needs met were guided by those values. As a bonus, their frequency of sexual intercourse increased to once every three weeks or so. That still wasn't as often as Maria would have preferred, but their relationship was ever so much better, and both were much more content than before.

Other Ways to Meet Our Needs

Many of us expect too much from our partner. Among other things, we may expect them to meet our needs emotionally, psychologically, and sexually; be romantic; be our confidant; give us security; make our life meaningful and purposeful; do housework; raise the kids; shop and cook; earn money; pay bills; fix and maintain things around the house; entertain and amuse us; spend time with extended family...and the list goes on and on. There's just no way one person can realistically meet all our needs, wants, and desires. With all that pressure and expectation, it's hardly surprising so many relationships collapse.

Therefore, it's important to know when to back off and look at other ways to meet your needs. Let's revisit Antonio and Maria. The way I described it makes it sound like it was all smooth sailing. But it wasn't. Maria initially came to therapy by herself because Antonio wasn't interested. From his perspective, she was "the one with the problem" and she needed to "back off and give him some space." So initially I worked just with Maria, and we brainstormed ways she could get her needs met *without* relying on Antonio. She recognized she could be sensual and intimate *with herself*, and achieve sexual pleasure through masturbation. She could connect deeply *with herself* through journaling, meditation, or yoga. And she could meet her needs for love, affection and connection through building close, intimate relationships with friends and family.

Her first reaction to this was an angry protest: "But that's not the same as having sex!"

I agreed with her. I said, "You're right. It's not the same thing at all. There's a huge gap here between the reality you've got and the reality you want. So what feelings would expect *anybody* to have in the face of such a reality gap?"

"Frustration!" she replied.

"Absolutely," I said. "Frustration. Disappointment. Sadness. Anger. These are all normal feelings, given the circumstances. You can't stop them showing up. The question is, what's the best way to respond to them: OBEY? STRUGGLE? Or drop anchor, make room, and be kind to yourself?"

Fortunately, Maria chose the latter response, and for several months she focused on getting her needs met outside the relationship. She stopped pressuring Antonio and instead, gently applied the principles of positive reinforcement (catch them doing it right, carrot versus stick, active appreciation). Over time, the tension between them reduced and Antonio eventually agreed to come to a therapy session, which is when we had the joint brainstorming session I described earlier.

So when your partner can't or won't *willingly* meet your needs, first drop anchor. Unhook from unhelpful stories, make room for those painful feelings, and practice lots of self-compassion. Then consider:

- Is it genuinely important to keep pursuing this with my partner, or is it just sucking the life out of our relationship? Could it be healthier and wiser to look at alternative ways to meet this need?

- If my partner is currently unable or unwilling, is there any way I can satisfy this need myself?

- Can I meet this need through other relationships, such as those with my family and friends?

Sticky Situations

What if you've used all the communication, assertiveness, and negotiation strategies we've covered and you're still stuck? For example:

- One partner wants children, but the other doesn't.

- One partner wants to live overseas, but the other doesn't.

- One partner wants to get married, but the other doesn't.

These are sticky, complicated, painful, messy situations, and they don't' have simple answers. As the writer H. L. Mencken put it, "For every complex problem there is an answer that is clear, simple, and wrong." Now your mind does not like this idea. It will often go into overdrive, trying desperately to find a solution: analyze, analyze, analyze; ponder, ponder, ponder. But your mind is unlikely to be successful. Don't take my word for it: check your experience. If you are currently in a sticky situation, consider this: How much time have you spent trying to resolve it? How much time have you wasted inside-the-mind—worrying, stewing, ruminating, obsessing, analyzing, or brooding? And what effect is that having on you, your partner, and your relationship?

The harsh reality is this: *Sticky situations don't have easy answers!* Life has dumped this problem on your doorstep. You didn't expect it; you didn't ask for it; you didn't want it. It's difficult, it's painful, and it's unfair. Yet here it is. This is your current reality, and you can't send it back. So can you practice self-compassion?

The larger the gap between what you want and what you've got, the more painful the feelings that arise and the more unhelpful things your mind will say. We can't stop these thoughts and feelings from showing up. They are normal human reactions. But we *can* drop anchor amidst our emotional storms. We *can* make room for painful feelings and be kind to ourselves. And we *can* still live by our values, do things that are meaningful, and engage in what we are doing. That doesn't solve the problem or get rid of the pain, but it enables us to live a meaningful life while making room for our pain.

And can you extend that compassion to your partner? Openly acknowledge how hard this situation is? Reveal to each other how much you are hurting? Can you acknowledge your partner's pain, and think and act kindly toward them, knowing they are hurting just like you? When you fell in love, you never anticipated this issue. Now you're both suffering. Neither of you wanted this. Both of you need and deserve some care and kindness. And in addition, it's useful to consider...

CHAPTER 17

Making Repairs

It is World War I, the winter of 1914. The Germans have been fighting the British and French for five long months, and hundreds of thousands have died on both sides. Imagine you're a British soldier on the battlefields of Flanders, Belgium. You're cold, wet, hungry, dirty, exhausted; you're living in a muddy trench infested with rats; you're a long way from home and frightened of dying.

It's December 24, and as the night grows dark and bitterly cold, you can't believe tomorrow is Christmas Day. Suddenly you see a glow above the German trenches. You can't believe your eyes. It's a Christmas tree, decorated with candles. And the Germans are singing carols that you recognize—the words are German, but the tunes are exactly the same!

In his book *Silent Night: The Story of the World War I Christmas Truce*, Stanley Weintraub describes what happened next: "After a few trees were shot at, the British became more curious than belligerent and crawled forward to watch and listen. And after a while, they began to sing. By Christmas morning, the 'no man's land' between the trenches was filled with fraternizing soldiers, sharing rations and gifts, singing and (more solemnly) burying their dead between the lines. Soon they were even playing soccer" (Weintraub 2001).

"The Christmas Truce" has to be one of the most amazing episodes in human history. Rival armies that had been killing each other mercilessly for months put down their weapons, climbed out of their trenches, and made friends. They sang songs and exchanged gifts; shared cigarettes, chocolate cake, and cognac; they played soccer on frozen mud with empty food cans. Sadly, the truce didn't last more than a few days. But that does not detract from the astonishing nature of this event. It shows us that even in the midst of a war zone, there is always the potential to connect with your core values.

Patching Up

We can all learn from this story. At times, we get so embroiled in conflict with our partner that we lose touch with our heart. Armed to the teeth with anger, resentment, and bitterness, we charge into battle, intent on winning at any cost. Or we huddle up in our trench, miserable, lonely, and exhausted.

Yet, at any moment, we can declare a truce. We can stop attacking, defending, detouring, or withdrawing, and instead reach out caringly toward our partner, and make a genuine attempt to repair the damage. The more we do this, the better for both partners. Each attempt we make to stop the fight, reach out, and patch up sends the message, "I care about you; I don't want to fight; I want us to have a good relationship!"

The term "repair attempt" means any words, actions, or gestures intended to repair the relationship. Earlier I mentioned John Gottman. His extensive research shows that even when couples fight a lot, if they're good at repairing, their relationship can still be healthy (Gottman and Silver 1999).

However, it's not just the sending that matters; it's also the receiving. If you are mindful of these reparative words and gestures—if you consciously notice and appreciate them—that enables bonding and healing. But if your partner reaches out and you push them away—if you close off, or keep attacking, or deflect, dismiss, or ignore their attempts to make up—then bonding and healing are not possible. Instead, the wounds grow deeper.

There are many ways to send a repair attempt. Here are a few to get you thinking:

Reveal you're in pain. One way to stop the battle is simply by taking off your armor to show you're wounded. You could say, "Ouch," "I'm really hurting now," "I'm getting a headache," "I'm getting really stressed," "I'm feeling scared," or "I'm feeling overwhelmed."

Ask for "time-out." We discussed this strategy in chapter 13. You could say: "Can we please take a rest?" "I can't handle this. I need a break." "How about we take time-out?" "Can we agree to disagree?"

Ask for better conditions. Another option is to continue the discussion but change the fighting conditions. For example: "Can you please lower your voice?" "I'm happy to discuss this, but please don't yell." "That felt like it was below the belt. Can we please fight fairly here?" "Please stick to the topic." "Can you please say that again without all the judgments?"

Acknowledge the pointlessness. You might comment on the fact that the fighting is getting you nowhere, for example: "This is pointless, isn't it? We're getting nowhere." "How much longer are we going to fight over this?"

Use humor. Many unhooking techniques can be used with a dose of humor, for example: "I think my inner shark just got out." "We're stuck in the 'I'm right, you're wrong' story." "Uh oh! We're hooked!"

Aim to understand. As discussed in chapter 14, we can often improve the situation by making a concerted effort to see it from the other's perspective and understand their needs and their feelings. We might say, "I don't understand where you're coming from. Please help me here," or "Let me see if I can get this from your point of view."

Offer an apology. When we get hooked by "I'm right, you're wrong," apologizing is often the last thing we want to do. Because of this, it can be very powerful and healing. We might say: "I'm sorry. I didn't mean to hurt you." "I'm sorry. I really screwed up badly." "Can we just press rewind here, and start again?" "I didn't intend it to come out like that. I take that back." "I did it again, didn't I? Sorry." Note: It needs to be a genuine apology. For tips on avoiding insincere apologies—like "I'm sorry you feel that way"—and how to give genuine impactful apologies, see "Extra Bits."

Make amends. Following your apology, offer to make amends. "How can I set this right?" "What can I do to make up here?" Better still, don't ask, just do it: actively do something to compensate. Make them a cup of coffee, buy a gift, organize a special event, take over a chore, cook a meal, do that thing you've been promising to do, and so on.

Unhooking Comes First

It's hard to effectively send or receive a repair attempt if you're trapped inside-the-mind, or powering along in reactive mode. So drop anchor, notice and name the story, make room for your feelings, get present, and connect with your values. With practice, this only takes a few seconds. It's like pressing the pause button during a movie; for a few moments, everything stops in its tracks. And that few seconds is all the time you need to make a difference. Pause, get present, reset. Then engage again with a values-guided response.

The same holds true on the receiving end. If you're lost in your psychological smog, you won't be able to see what your partner is doing. There they are, waving the white flag, but you just keep on shooting. You may need to unhook from stories like *She doesn't mean this,* or *This is his way of having a go at me,* or *Don't think you can get out of it that easily!* And if you spot anything that looks even remotely like a repair attempt, no matter how vague or fuzzy it seems through the smog, then acknowledge it: perhaps with a smile, or a nod of your head, or by saying something like: "Thanks," "I appreciate that," "Fair call," or "I'm sorry, too." This doesn't come naturally for most of us, but it's an essential part of building a strong relationship.

And of course, there will be occasions when you forget everything in this book, and you get entangled in a nasty fight. (This happens to all of us at times—including the author!) Still, the moment you realize what's happened, there's a choice point. One option is DRAIN (disconnection, reactivity, avoidance, inside-the-mind, neglecting values). The other is: drop anchor and make repairs.

If Your Partner Is Willing

The list of repair attempts is by no means exhaustive. Brainstorm what you could say or do to de-escalate a conflict, and help you to recover and repair.

Think back over old conflicts; was there anything you said or did that helped reduce the damage, or repair it?

Agree on some words, phrases, or physical gestures you can use in the future to make repair attempts.

Make a pact to be mindful of each other's repair attempts: to acknowledge them and accept them, even when you feel angry, hurt, or resentful.

A Word of Caution

Any and all of these techniques can backfire if your partner takes your words or gestures the wrong way. So make it clear that you're trying to patch things up. If necessary, spell it out literally: "I'm trying to patch things up" or even "This is a repair attempt." Also be honest with yourself; if you're not mindful of your own intentions, you can easily subvert some of these comments into attacks, digs, jibes, and put-downs. So as you try these strategies, stay in touch with your values around being caring and considerate.

Compassion for Your Partner

Back in chapter 10 we looked at the concept and practice of self-compassion: *acknowledging your pain and responding with kindness*. We focused on self-compassion as a way of supporting ourselves when we're hurting. Now let's consider the equally important topic of compassion for other people: *acknowledging the pain of others and responding with kindness*. If we turn a blind eye to the pain and suffering of our partner—ignore it, dismiss it, or simply fail to notice it—what happens? Does it bring us closer together, or push us further apart?

Without compassion, it becomes easy to judge others, look down on them, scorn them, neglect them, reject them, or hurt them. And what effect does that have on our relationships?

So as well as practicing self-compassion, it's wise to practice compassion for your partner. In chapter 4, I asked you to reflect on how your partner has been suffering. We're going to end this chapter with a similar exercise—but this time, we'll go further. (Note: As you do this exercise, your mind may protest: *They don't deserve my compassion!* If so, you know what to do.)

EXERCISE: Compassion for Your Partner

Ideally, use the free audio in "Extra Bits" (chapter 17) as your guide through this exercise. If that doesn't suit, please follow the written instructions.

Take a few minutes to reflect on your partner and how they have been suffering. What's it like for them when you're disconnected, reactive, or using destructive tactics? What's it like for them when you push them away, withdraw, judge, or criticize? (If you're finding this hard to imagine, consider what's it like when you get treated that way; how do you feel? Your partner's probably feeling something similar.)

Get a sense of their pain: their anger, sadness, fear, loneliness, guilt, shame, or despair. Do you wish them to suffer in this way?

Remember, just like you, they came into this relationship wanting to love and be loved, wanting to care and be cared for, hoping to enrich and improve their life. No one enters a relationship because they want to quarrel with or hurt the other person.

Just like you, your partner gets repeatedly hooked by difficult thoughts and feelings, pulled away from their values, and jerked into destructive patterns of behavior. And just like you, they hurt and suffer as a result.

So take a moment to acknowledge: your partner is suffering.

See if you can tap into a sense of kindness. A good way to do this is to imagine your partner in pain: hooked, hurting, and struggling. Imagine yourself reaching out to them, with genuine kindness and caring.

You may imagine yourself talking to them with kind and understanding words, touching them in a kind and comforting way, or doing some sort of kind, supportive deed.

Or you may imagine this in a more abstract way: sending kind energy, kind vibes, kind feelings to your partner. (However you imagine this is fine; you might visualize it, think about it, feel it, or sense it.)

And as you do this, silently say to your partner: *I see you're in pain. I care about you. I want to help. I don't want you to suffer. I want you to experience love, caring, and kindness. I want to make this work.*

Take a few moments to sit with this experience, and notice what happens. All sorts of feelings may arise; some may be "warm and fuzzy," while others may be very unpleasant. Allow your feelings to be as they are; notice and name them, make room for them, and actively bring some kindness to yourself.

Finally, end the exercise by dropping anchor.

Many people find this exercise is quite challenging, but also, usually, helpful. So if it was helpful for you, please run through it on a regular basis. Even a "quickie" is useful: take just one minute to acknowledge your partner is hurting and send them some kind energy or silently say a few kind words. Remember back in chapter 13 we discussed how to have a constructive "time-out"? Well, during that time-out period, if you can tap into some compassion for your partner, it's sure to be helpful.

Of course, the ultimate aim with this practice is to turn it into action. If you're only compassionate inside your head, that won't do much for your relationship. So translate your compassion into words and actions. What compassionate things can you say and do? Consider what words, deeds, and gestures will convey the three central messages: *I see you're in pain; I care about you; I'm here for you.*

Although this practice is challenging, it's well worth making the effort, because it paves the way for genuine...

CHAPTER 18

Intimacy

What's it all about? Why bother working on your relationship? What does it really matter? These are big questions, and there are no "right" answers. However, for most people, one major factor is the desire to be truly known and genuinely accepted. When someone sees us as we truly are behind all our pretenses, behind the show we put on for the world around us, behind that mask we wear in everyday life, and if, having seen our flaws, failings, and weaknesses, they continue to accept us and care for us, then we feel genuinely and deeply loved.

Allowing someone to "know the real you" is commonly called "intimacy." The word comes from the Latin *intimatio*, which means "to make known." It refers to a deep and close connection between two human beings. We can talk about intimacy in at least three ways:

Physical intimacy: letting your partner know your body

Emotional intimacy: letting your partner know your feelings

Psychological intimacy: letting your partner know what's on your mind, including your values, goals, needs, opinions, beliefs, expectations, and fantasies

The deepest, closest relationships usually involve intimacy in all three areas. (However, this is not always so. It's important to remember that each couple is unique, and there is no set formula as to what is "normal." Always look at what works to enrich and deepen your own unique relationship, as opposed to what the "experts" say is normal.)

Genuine Intimacy: An Act of Willingness

Intimacy is a two-way street. For a true intimate connection, each of you needs to "make yourself known" to your partner. This cannot be forced or coerced. Genuine intimacy is an act of willingness; you willingly allow your partner to know you emotionally, physically, or psychologically. If you do this grudgingly or resentfully, or out of a sense of coercion or guilt or fear, it would be a destructive experience.

Taking a Risk

To open up emotionally and psychologically is to take a risk. If you tell your partner how you are feeling or what you are thinking, you make yourself vulnerable, open yourself to attack. For example, your partner could criticize you. They could slap harsh judgments upon you, express their disapproval, or ridicule and mock you. They might even use that information to try to manipulate you or to deliberately hurt you.

Hopefully these things will not happen, but there's no guarantee. Indeed, some of those things may have already happened—either in your current relationship or in previous ones. So when you open up to your partner, you are taking a risk. And when humans take risks, they feel anxious (or fearful, edgy, uneasy, nervous, tense, unsafe, insecure—whatever you prefer to call it). So the question is, are you willing to make room for those feelings in order to build a closer, deeper relationship?

If your answer is no, then your relationship will inevitably lack intimacy. If your answer is yes, consider how you can minimize any risks. There's no point in being foolhardy or impetuous.

Making It Safe

One way to minimize the risk involved in intimacy is to move slowly, take "baby steps," and observe how your partner responds. Think about tiny ways in which you might be a bit more intimate. Perhaps you might use "I" statements to share your feelings: "I'm worried about XYZ," or "I feel very in love with you." Or perhaps you might disclose a genuine opinion rather than holding your tongue or saying something you don't really believe. Or you might tell your partner some of your dreams or hopes, rather than hiding them.

As you take these risks, notice your partner's reactions. If they respond with openness, curiosity, caring, and consideration, those are good signs. If they respond with hostility, contempt, disinterest, or rejection, those are bad signs: red flags that usually indicate the need for professional help from a therapist or relationship counselor.

The same holds true when the shoe is on the other foot. Make it safe for your partner to open up to you. Apply the principles of good communication: be present, open, and curious; connect with your values of loving and caring; and adjust your voice, face, and posture to convey warmth and openness. By making a "safe space" for your partner to open up and "be real" with you, you contribute to their health and well-being, as well as building a deep connection between you.

Validating Your Partner's Feelings

At times, you and your partner *will* see eye-to-eye; you will have similar opinions and similar feelings about a particular issue. When this happens, you both feel united, aligned, supported. At other times, however, this will not be the case. The likelihood is that you and your partner will have differing opinions and feelings about a wide variety of subjects, issues, and situations. When this happens, watch out for "I'm right, you're wrong." If you let that story hook you, you know where it leads.

To *validate* your partner's feelings doesn't mean you *agree* with them. It means you understand that this is how your partner thinks and feels right now; and even though you think and feel differently, you respect their right to have their own individual thoughts and feelings. You cultivate an attitude of acceptance: "Your thoughts and feelings are different from mine; I may not like that difference, but I am willing to accommodate it."

Naturally you will judge your partner's thoughts and feelings—to do so is human nature—but you don't hold on tightly to those judgments. You let them come and go like passing cars. And instead you make peace with the reality that this is how your partner feels and thinks. It's hardly surprising they think or feel differently to you: after all, you're two different people. And if you knew your partner in intimate detail, including their genetic and biological makeup, the structure of their brain and nervous system, the complete history of each and every relationship they've ever had, and all the formative learning experiences they've had throughout their life—if you had that knowledge, then the thoughts and feelings your partner has would seem perfectly natural and normal—even though they may be wildly different from your own.

"Validation" means you convey to your partner that it's all right for them to have their own unique thoughts and feelings—even when they're radically different to yours. If you're not willing to do this—if you cling to the story that your partner *shouldn't* feel or think as they do—then what does this cost you? What impact does it have on your relationship?

Validation is an important act of caring. It doesn't mean you agree with your partner; it doesn't mean you like or approve of the way they think and feel; it means you see and hear them, and allow them to be who they are.

If you start attacking, criticizing, judging, challenging, minimizing, dismissing, or ignoring your partner's thoughts and feelings, this is "invalidating." Invalidating your partner's feelings is hurtful and destructive; it destroys trust and prevents intimacy. Invalidating comments may include: *What's the big deal? What are you getting so upset about? It's no use crying over spilt milk. Cheer up, it may never happen. You're so negative! Let's be rational about this.* These comments all send the same message: there's something wrong with your feelings (and there's something wrong with you for having them).

Invalidation comes in many forms. Suppose your partner admits to making a mistake with painful consequences. A validating response might be: *Ouch, that must hurt. But hey, you're human. We all make mistakes. Go easy on yourself.* An invalidating response might be: *Well, that was a stupid thing to do.* Or: *Well, you've only got yourself to blame.*

Unsolicited advice can also frequently invalidate. Suppose that we immediately launch into problem-solving and giving advice, without first acknowledging our partner's suffering. If so, our partner may well feel invalidated, as if their feelings aren't important.

Also watch out for statements like this: *If I were in your shoes, then I'd be doing XYZ.* Or: *If I were in your situation, I wouldn't be feeling A, I'd be feeling B.* At first glance, this may seem empathic, as if you're putting yourself in your partner's shoes. But it's not really. What you're really saying is this: *If I were in your situation, with my biology, my brain, my childhood, my upbringing, my history of relationships, my skills, my knowledge, and my life experiences, then I would do XYZ.* In other words: *If you were me, you'd know better!* To really understand your partner's feelings and choices, you need to truly imagine what it's like to be *them,* not *you.* You need to consider: *If I were in your situation, with your biology, your brain, your childhood, your upbringing, your history of relationships, your skills, your knowledge, and your life experiences…then I would do the same things or have the same feelings, or think about things the same way that you do.*

To validate your partner's thoughts and feelings, you will not only need to let go of righteous ideas or judgments but also make room for your own discomfort. Quite often, as your partner reveals their inner world, you'll experience uncomfortable feelings, from anxiety and impatience to frustration or guilt. Your challenge is to switch off STRUGGLE mode and, instead, make room for your discomfort. (This is communication principle number two: open up.)

And when your partner reveals painful feelings, validation is an important aspect of compassion. You might say things like:

"Ouch. That must hurt."

"It's natural you'd feel that way."

"This must be really hard for you."

"Tell me more."

"I'm here for you."

"This is tough for you. How can I help?"

These are just a few ideas. Why not discuss with your partner what you'd each find validating? Validation pays big dividends over time. Not least of which is...

Building a Better Sex Life

Many people arbitrarily divide their relationship up into two parts: 1) their sex life and 2) everything else. This division is often unhelpful. It's more useful to think of sex as merely one activity that allows you to connect in a pleasurable way. Some people expect that despite a terrible relationship full of DRAIN and destructive tactics—they should be able to have a great sex life. Think again! Almost always, the greater the tension and conflict in your relationship, the worse your sex life will be. After all, if you can't connect lovingly outside the bedroom, why should it be any different inside?

Generally speaking, if your sex life isn't good, first focus on reversing the DRAIN in nonsexual aspects of your relationship. As you reestablish caring, connection, compassion, and trust, this opens the door to a better, more enjoyable sex life. But if you attempt to do it the other way around—to fix up your sex life while your relationship is going down the gurgler—your chances of success are minimal. Once your relationship is thriving outside the bedroom, then you can focus on your sex life.

Sex and Unhooking from Unhelpful Thoughts

To enhance your sex life, what unhelpful expectations, rules, and judgments could you unhook from? Here are some common ones:

- Your partner should like (or at least consent to) the same sexual activities as you.

- You or your partner should want to have sex more often/less often.

- You or your partner should have a stronger erection or orgasm.

- You or your partner should get an erection or reach an orgasm more easily/more often/more quickly/more slowly.

If these "shoulds" hook you, you'll repeatedly experience anxiety, frustration, or disappointment. Why? Because orgasms, erections, personal tastes, and sex drive all vary enormously—not only from person to person but from week to week and day to day. So if you grasp those expectations tightly, you'll be struggling with reality.

The same goes for "I'm right, you're wrong," which often takes the guise of "I'm normal, you're abnormal"—especially when it comes to foreplay, sexual positions, masturbation, sex toys, or the "when, where, and how" of what you do. And let's not forget all those judgments about performance, technique, and physical appearance.

It's natural to have these rules, expectations, and judgments, but don't let them hook you. Notice them, name them, and hold them lightly, or the smog will be so thick, you won't even be able to see your bedroom!

Sex and Negotiation

Remember Maria and Antonio (chapter 16)? Maria wanted sex weekly, but Antonio wanted it monthly. To resolve the issue, they shelved their conflicting goals and looked instead at their underlying needs: connection, caring, intimacy, affection, and sensuality. You can use the same strategy with your own sex life. If you communicate well, negotiate fairly, and you're willing to compromise if necessary, then you can usually find many ways to make it work. However, make sure to honor your values of self-care and self-respect. Remember: intimacy is an act of willingness. If your partner is trying to coerce or manipulate you into doing something against your will, that's not intimacy! So be assertive: in a fair and considerate manner, ask for what you want and decline anything you don't wish to do.

Sex and "Making Room"

When you're trying out new things, rediscovering old things, or having sex after a long absence, there's a high chance you'll feel anxious, vulnerable, tense, embarrassed, or uncomfortable—at least initially. So are you willing to make room for those feelings in the service of better sex and more intimacy?

Sex and Values

Many people ruin their sex lives by turning sex into a goal—focused activity: all about the orgasm. While having an orgasm is generally a pleasurable experience, if it becomes "the be all and end all" of your sex life, sooner or later this attitude creates problems. Why? Because inevitably there will be times when you or your partner will not get aroused, or achieve orgasm, or get an erection; or you'll come too quickly, or slowly, or not at all. Common reasons include tiredness, stress, anxiety, depression, physical illness, drugs, alcohol, effects of aging—and ongoing DRAIN in your relationship. And sometimes it even happens for no good reason—"just because."

Here's a common story that many cling to: "The main point of sex is to reach orgasm—and it's not good sex unless that happens!" If we hold this story tightly, it creates an intense atmosphere where there's real pressure to perform and achieve your goal. This in turn leads to "performance anxiety": a feeling of stress, pressure, or fear of failure linked to sexual intercourse. And the problem is, our sexual organs typically "switch off" when we're stressed or anxious, making it almost impossible to reach orgasm, control ejaculation, or keep an erection. So the more pressure you feel to "perform," the more likely you are to have sexual problems. Spot the vicious cycle, anyone? Before long, one or both partners start avoiding sex altogether because it becomes so fraught with unpleasant feelings!

If you make your sex life values-focused rather than goal-focused, you can break this vicious cycle. Instead of focusing on erections and orgasms, you can use sex as a way to live your values: for example, being loving, caring, open, attentive, intimate, affectionate, or sensual. And notice you can live these values in many ways, whether or not you achieve the goal of orgasm. With this attitude, you are free.

Sex and Mindfulness

Mindfulness can wonderfully enhance physical intimacy. Whether you're kissing, hugging, caressing, nuzzling, holding hands, stroking, undressing, embracing, or having foreplay, oral sex, or intercourse, mindfulness can intensify both the pleasure and the sense of deep connection. When you tune into the sensations in your own body and simultaneously tune into the reactions of your partner, sex becomes an absorbing and engaging experience—far more pleasurable than when you're all caught up in your thoughts or excessively focused on achieving the goal of orgasm.

Plenty of Options

If we define "intimacy" broadly to include all three components—physical, emotional, and psychological—there are many ways of building it: talking about your feelings, sharing your hopes and dreams, cuddling, discussing your philosophy of life, holding hands, revealing your deepest fears, kissing passionately, having a bath together, sharing fond memories, having intercourse, planning a holiday. Provided both partners are open, engaged, and caring, the opportunities for intimacy are endless; all you need is to use your imagination.

CHAPTER 19

Giving Back to Yourself

We all get hurt in life. Sometimes others hurt us intentionally: perhaps out of racism, sexism, prejudice, competitiveness, or revenge. Or perhaps out of anger, or cruelty, or the desire to impress others. However, very often, others hurt us unintentionally: out of anxiety, insecurity, envy, jealousy, or sheer ignorance.

Ignorance is a big factor in hurting others. Think about how often you have unintentionally hurt someone you truly care about by saying or doing something that you never expected to be hurtful. Lack of awareness is another common culprit. How often have you upset or hurt someone simply because you did not pay attention to what you were doing and how it was affecting them? Or because you were so caught up in your own thoughts and feelings that you were unaware of theirs?

Regardless of the motivation, whenever somebody hurts us, we feel pain. And if we respond in OBEY or STRUGGLE mode, that usually just magnifies it. For example, we may get angry about what happened and take it out on the people around us, often hurting others in the process. Or we may replay those painful memories over and over, hurting ourselves repeatedly to no avail. Or we may hatch revenge fantasies, which only fuel our anger and resentment. Or we may drink, smoke, eat junk food, take drugs, and so on.

Our mind says things like: *Why me? How could this happen? This isn't fair! I don't deserve this.* If the nature of the hurt was major, your mind may even claim that you'll never get over it; that you are irreparably damaged by what has happened; or perhaps that you even deserved it! One thing's for sure: if you get hooked by these stories, they rapidly suck you dry of health and vitality. Especially if you get hooked by resentment.

The word "resentment" comes from the French *resentir*, which means "to feel again." When hooked by resentment, we relive the pain of that old hurt, over and over again. Instead of healing the wound, we open it up and rub salt in it. In Alcoholics Anonymous, there's a saying: resentment is like drinking poison and hoping that the other person dies. In other words, in the grip of resentment, it's you getting hurt, not the person who wronged you.

The Antidote

The antidote to resentment is "forgiveness." But ACT has an interesting take on that idea. You see, "forgiveness" is derived from the words "give" and "before." It means "*giving* yourself back what was there *before* resentment took over." In other words, "bad stuff" happens, you get hurt, and what you're left with now is resentment. But what was life like *before* resentment hooked you? More peace of mind? More contentment? More living in the present, rather than reliving the past? "Forgiveness" means giving this back to yourself. It's something you do *purely for yourself*, to improve your own health and well-being.

Importantly:

- It doesn't mean forgetting, excusing, pardoning, trivializing, or justifying any of the bad stuff that happened.

- It doesn't mean you *have to* say or do anything to the other person involved (although you can if you want to).

- It is to relieve your own suffering and free you up to build a better life.

Forgiveness requires all your mindfulness skills. When painful thoughts and memories show up, you notice them, name them, and refocus. If you get pulled into the stream of resentment, you notice it and step back out again.

If painful feelings—anger, sadness, betrayal—arise, you make room for them, and practice self-compassion. If a massive storm of resentment blows up, you drop anchor.

You then connect with your values. You remind yourself, "That was in the past; what do I want to do *now?*" You then translate your values into actions: you start doing something meaningful and engage fully in whatever that may be. And that, folks, is forgiveness! Following is an exercise to help you with this process. (And yes, there's a copy in "Extra Bits.")

EXERCISE: How to Forgive

Please carefully complete the following statements:

1. When I get hooked by blame, judgment, or resentment toward my partner, and pulled into reliving what they did, the effect that has on me is

   _____

2. At times, when hooked by those thoughts, feelings, and memories, I have done things that made my life worse, such as

   _____

   _____

3. And what that has cost me is

   _____

   _____

4. So for my own health and well-being, I choose to practice unhooking from blame, judgment, and resentment. The methods I will use are

   _____

   _____

5. And when difficult memories arise, I will acknowledge the pain and be kind to myself, as follows:

_____

_____

I will also reflect regularly on the following:

- What my partner did to hurt me gave rise to much pain and suffering.

- It was not okay. I will not forget it.

- If I knew my partner inside out, knew their whole life history, I would understand why they did this. But I will never know for sure why they did what they did—and I don't need to.

- The fact is we all screw up, make mistakes, and do things that hurt others.

- The fact is we all at times get hooked by thoughts and feelings and pulled into destructive patterns of behavior.

- My partner is imperfect and fallible, prone to human weakness and error—just as I am.

- My partner gets hooked by their own thoughts and feelings and pulled into destructive patterns of behavior—just as I do.

- My partner did what they did, and I can't change that, but I can unhook from unhelpful thoughts and practice self-compassion; I will continue to do so, in the interest of building a better life for myself.

———————————————————————

If Your Partner Is Willing

Many couples find it healing to create their own forgiveness ritual. Following are the basic elements, but please use your creativity to make it more personal.

Step 1: Each partner writes a letter that completes these three sentences:

- The thoughts, feelings, and memories I've been getting hooked by are:

- Getting hooked by all this has hurt our relationship in the following ways:

- I want to build a better relationship, based on the following values:

Step 2: At the end of the letter, each partner writes in their own words some sort of commitment to unhook from all these painful thoughts and feelings.

Step 3: Choose a special place and read your letters aloud to each other. This could be anywhere from a special room in your house, to a park or a beach. As one partner reads, the other listens mindfully and compassionately.

Step 4: Do something that symbolizes starting over—for example, burn the letters and scatter the ashes.

Step 5: Do something to connect lovingly—for example, kiss, hug, go out to dinner, light a candle, and listen to music you both love.

What About Trust?

Forgiveness is not trust. If your partner has deceived, betrayed, or misled you, then trust can take a loooong time to rebuild. So let's consider what's needed for...

CHAPTER 20

Building a Trust Fund

"How could he do that to me?"

"Why did I believe her?"

"Why didn't I see it coming?"

"How can I ever trust again?"

When someone you love deceives or betrays you, it hurts. Badly. And the wounds take a long time to heal. If your partner has cheated, lied, deceived, betrayed, manipulated, or harmed you, you'll need to make a tough choice about whether to continue your relationship. This choice is never easy, and will depend on many factors, including children, finances, mitigating circumstances, the nature of the betrayal, whether it has happened before, and whether your partner is taking responsibility and making amends. So make sure to practice plenty of self-compassion while you take the time necessary to make this difficult decision. Acknowledge your pain and stress—and be kind to yourself.

Blind Trust versus Mindful Trust

If you do choose to stay (at least for now), you have some hard work ahead of you. When you've been hurt, abused, or deceived by a person you trust deeply, it takes a long time to feel safe and secure with them again. So if you *do* choose to stay, you can expect to have plenty of thoughts and feelings of suspicion, insecurity, doubt, jealousy, or anxiety. And if you want your relationship to survive, recover, and thrive, are you willing to make room for those feelings while doing the hard work of rebuilding trust?

If your answer is no, then you are stuck; and you will remain stuck until you either leave the relationship or commit to working on it; in which case, practice lots of self-compassion, because that's a very painful situation to be stuck in.

However, if your answer is yes, you are willing to do the hard work of rebuilding, then it's important to distinguish between blind trust and mindful trust. "Blind trust" means you trust someone without bothering to assess whether they deserve it. "Mindful trust" means you carefully notice what this person says and does, and trust them only if they earn it. In particular, consider:

- Is your partner honest, or do they tend to lie?

- Is your partner open, or do they tend to hide things?

- Is your partner reliable? Do they follow through on their promises?

- Is your partner considerate? Do they consider your needs, your rights, your feelings?

- Is your partner responsible? Do they willingly own up to their "bad behavior" and make amends? Or do they dismiss it, deny it, excuse it, or lie about it? Or try to avoid discussing it through aggression, withdrawal, silence, accusation, or gaslighting?

Obviously, there's no such thing as the perfect partner; no one is *always* honest, open, reliable, considerate, and responsible. We're human beings, not superheroes. However, if your partner *generally* exhibits these qualities, *and* maintains them over the long haul, then *over time*, they may prove themselves "trustworthy." The key point: don't blindly give them your trust; let them earn it.

Also keep in mind, we can't control the *feelings* of trust; we can only control the actions. So if you *do* choose to start trusting your partner, begin with small actions: trust them in tiny little ways, carefully observe what happens, and see if they prove worthy.

If your partner proves trustworthy, then over time, you may be willing to take larger actions of trust—all the while, mindfully observing the consequences. Step by step, you can carry on doing this, while making room for those inevitable feelings of anxiety, insecurity, and doubt. And if your partner continues to respond appropriately, then perhaps, after a long while, you may again experience *feelings* of trust. (Trust isn't a feeling in the same sense as emotions like fear, anger, and sadness. It's more a deep sense of security.)

As you do all this, it's important to maintain a healthy balance between actions of self-protection and actions of trust. For example, if your partner has cheated on you, it's reasonable to call them at the office when they say they're working late. If your partner has frittered away your savings on gambling, it's reasonable to keep an eye on all the bank accounts. As trust is gradually reestablished, these self-protective actions become less necessary.

The key is to find a healthy balance that works for your relationship. If it's all about self-protection, you'll never repair and rebuild; but if it's all about trust and you neglect self-protection, you're taking foolish risks. So find a balance that works and expect it to shift gradually over time (assuming your partner continues to prove trustworthy). And be realistic about time frames; this may take many months or even years.

Finally, acknowledge: you can never have certainty. If you want absolute certainty that your partner will never again deceive or betray you, the only way to ensure it is to end the relationship. So if you *do* choose to stay, uncertainty will come along for the ride. You can expect the recurrence of thoughts like "I'll get hurt again," and those knots in your stomach, and that tightness in your chest, and so on. Make room for those thoughts and feelings, but don't ignore them—use them as reminders to look out for yourself and avoid "blind trust."

If You've Betrayed Your Partner

If you have betrayed, deceived, or manipulated your partner, you'll have to work hard to regain their trust. You'll have to prove yourself to be honest, open, reliable, responsible, and considerate—and not just once or twice, but over and over again. And you'll need to make room for your partner's natural suspicion and reluctance to trust you again. You'll also need to unhook from stories like "She should have gotten over it by now" or "Why is he taking so long to trust me again?" It may take many months or years before you rebuild the trust fund. So are you willing to cultivate patience and persistence?

At times, when you see your partner's pain, you may feel anxious, sad, or guilty. Are you willing to make room for those feelings? To breathe into them, open up around them, and engage fully with your partner; to stay present, rather than withdrawing?

This is important. If you're not willing to make room for those painful feelings, you're bound to act in self-defeating ways. For example, you may try to push them away with anger. Anger feels empowering; we feel strong when we're angry. But it does not bode well for healing and repairing. Or you may try to suppress your feelings with drugs, food, or alcohol. This is obviously not good for your own health and well-being. Or you may try to distract yourself by getting very busy, watching TV, or scrolling through social media; this wastes a lot of time and does nothing constructive to repair your relationship. You may even try to avoid your partner because you don't like how you feel when you see their pain—but this would spell disaster in terms of rebuilding.

So instead of running from these feelings, actively use them. Your feelings contain important information, which you can use to connect with your values. Consider: What do your feelings tell you about what matters to you? What do they remind you that you need to address, face up to, or do differently? How can you translate that information into values-guided action?

You can also use these feelings to cultivate compassion—for both yourself and your partner. Yes, you deserve compassion, too! Beating yourself up will not alter the past or compensate for what happened. The more you practice self-compassion, the easier you'll find it to be compassionate toward your partner, which is something they truly need from you.

A Few Words on Temptation

At times, we all feel tempted to do things that we know will, in some way, hurt our partner. There is nothing "wrong" or "abnormal" about this; such thoughts, feelings, and urges are extremely common. They are only a problem if you respond in OBEY mode. If you let these thoughts and feelings dictate your actions, that might well lead to some short-term plea-sure—but in the long run, will it deepen and strengthen your relationship?

While you can't stop yourself from "feeling tempted," you can choose how you respond to those urges. You might *feel like* having sex with someone else, or gambling, or going on a drinking binge…but you don't *have to* do it! You can drop anchor, unhook, make room, get present, and exert conscious control over your actions. You can tune into your core relationship values, like being fair, loving, honest, and reliable. And you can base your actions on your values, rather than your urges.

In doing this consistently, you reap a double reward. Not only do you show your partner they can trust you, but you also build trust in yourself. Life will test you in a million different ways, so when you can truly trust yourself to respond wisely and effectively—well, that's a very precious gift.

CHAPTER 21

Time for Some Fun!

"All work and no play makes Jack a dull boy," so the proverb goes. Many of us neglect our values of being playful or humorous, and our needs for fun, and leisure, and entertainment. But without these elements, a relationship can become heavy, serious, or dull.

Creating Connection Rituals

Alas, in our busy, stressful lives, we can easily forget to make time for fun and games. So it's useful to set up regular "connection rituals." A *connection ritual* is any activity you do on a regular basis where the main purpose is to strengthen your bond with your partner. You can use these rituals to have fun, play games, share pleasure, support each other, express affection, or deepen intimacy. Simple connection rituals include:

- Talking about your day when you get home from work

- Having a heart-to-heart over a drink

- Going on a date: dinner, movies, bowling, dancing, and so on

- Sharing physical activities, such as running, swimming, walking, or yoga

- Sharing spiritual activities, such as meditation, prayer, or going to church

- Sharing hobbies, crafts, or creative activities

- Playing games

- Going on family outings

- Having friends over for dinner

- Being physically intimate

Making time to connect is vital for a healthy long-term relationship. So use this list to get you thinking, then pull out your journal, or use the "Extra Bits" worksheet, and jot down some ideas for your own rituals.

If Your Partner Is Willing

Jointly brainstorm ways in which you can connect more regularly. You can use the previous suggestions as a guide, and also think back on ways you connected in the past. Once you've generated a list, pick the best ideas, and plan when and where you will do them.

Many couples like to schedule a "date night." Once a week, you—just the two of you—go on a date. You don't socialize with friends, or bring children along; you appreciate spending time "one on one." If this idea appeals, pull out your calendar and write in the dates, at least a few weeks ahead. If you don't do this, then as you get caught up in the demands of daily life, your dates will be forgotten. (Obviously if once a week is not possible, adapt this idea to suit your own circumstances.)

Another ritual that many couples find helpful is a regular heart-to-heart talk about your relationship: a "check-in" to see how, from both points of view, the relationship is going. This could be something you do over dinner or a drink, or during a walk in the park, or even as part of your date night. Some couples do this every couple of weeks; others find once every month or two works better. You could try it out and adapt it to suit your needs. Here are some questions you might find useful during these talks:

- What's working in our relationship?

- What have you appreciated most in the last two weeks?

- When have you felt most connected, satisfied, loved, supported, understood, accepted, or cared for?

- What's not working? And what could we do differently that might work better?

When you plan dates or other connection rituals, think about ways to bring fun, games, leisure, and pleasure into your relationship. Taking turns, ask and answer these questions:

- What is your idea of fun?

- What makes you laugh, smile, or feel most alive?

- What do we do currently (and what have we done in the past) that is (or was) fun for you?

- How could we have more fun in the future?

Next, create some action plans: schedule some activities for fun and pleasure.

Keep Looking into Your Heart

ACT advocates that we reflect on our values regularly: think about them, talk about them, or write about them. This helps us to keep the "big picture" in mind: to stay in touch with what matters in the long run. When we're bogged down in unhelpful stories; hurting from fights and squabbles; disappointed or irritated by our partner's differences; feeling bored, trapped, disillusioned, or dissatisfied, we can always turn to our values for a helping hand: to lift us up and help us get back on track.

Our values, however, won't stack up neatly like books in a bookcase. They continuously move. Compare them to continents painted on a globe of the world: no matter how fast you spin that globe, in any given moment, there will always be some continents at the front, others at the back; you can't simultaneously see them all. But the ones at the back have not ceased to exist; they are just temporarily out of sight. And in different situations, some values will take priority over others; some will come to the front while others fall back.

In other words, we often need to shift between values, to suit the demands of the situation. To do this, we need to hold them lightly. Yes, values—just like any other thoughts—will create problems if we grasp them tightly; they turn into "rigid rules"—*should, must, have to!*—which are restrictive or oppressive. So come back to the notion of values as a compass. We want to pull out our compass from time to time, check that we're headed in the right direction; then put it away in our backpack until we need it again. We won't enjoy our journey if we're clutching the compass tightly each step of the way.

Wherever we go, whatever we do, our values are always with us. We can use them to guide and inspire us in any moment; to pull us out of the smog and into our life. So before you read on to the final chapter, I recommend you revisit chapter 5 and take a good, long look at what really matters. This will equip you well as...

CHAPTER 22

The Adventure Continues

Mark Twain once wrote, "To cease smoking is the easiest thing I ever did. I ought to know because I've done it a thousand times." Even if we've never smoked, most of us can relate to this witty observation. How often have you said, "I'm never going to do that again!" and sure enough, half an hour later you go and do it? How often have you thought, *Next time, I'm going to handle this differently!* And next time comes around and—*shock! horror!*—you end up doing the same old thing! The fact is, deeply entrenched behaviors are not that easy to stop. If you doubt this, take a good look at yourself: have you successfully eliminated all your "bad habits"? (If so, congratulations: you are the first perfect human being in history.)

Realism and Relapse

By the time your relationship is in trouble, both you and your partner will have many self-defeating habits—some of which you've had since childhood. Awareness of these habits is just the starting point. It's what comes next that makes the difference: the repeated practice and application of skills such as dropping anchor, noticing and naming, making room, self-compassion, being fully present, connecting with your values, good communication, and assertiveness.

Now time to be realistic. Whoever said "Practice makes perfect" was deluded. Practice will help you build better skills, but it won't permanently eliminate all your self-defeating behaviors. Both you and your partner will screw up, make mistakes, and fall back into "bad habits." This will happen again and again and again. It's part of being human.

But that doesn't mean you should "give up." It just means "be realistic." As Mark Twain famously said, "Habit is habit, and not to be flung out of the window by any man, but coaxed downstairs one step at a time." With practice, you can become much better at living by your values, emerging from your smog, engaging with your partner, negotiating fairly, making repairs, practicing forgiveness and compassion, being assertive, communicating clearly, expressing appreciation, and accepting your differences.

So the more you practice, the better the outlook for the future. At the same time, unhook from unrealistic expectations. Neither you nor your partner will always do what's best for the relationship. You're both imperfect, fallible human beings. And I guarantee there will be times when you forget everything in this book, and fall back into old ways.

That's why, when I counsel couples, I always discuss the inevitability of "relapse." I might say, "Okay, so she's just made a commitment that from now on, instead of yelling and criticizing, she'll explain calmly and respectfully why she's annoyed. Now I'm sure she's sincere; she seems genuinely determined to work on this. My question is, how likely is it that she will never, ever yell or criticize again?" In saying this, I'm not aiming to undermine the commitment; I am simply aiming to introduce some realism.

Most couples appreciate this. It helps them loosen their grip on the "perfect partner" story. Occasionally one partner protests, "No, that's not good enough. I need to know that it will never happen again." So I ask them to consider: If you hold on tightly to that expectation, does it strengthen or stress your relationship?

Obviously there are some types of behavior where relapse is not acceptable. If your partner has cheated on you, or betrayed you in other ways, then you may choose to leave rather than run the risk of a recurrence. Indeed, many people will advise you to do this. However, that's your decision, not anyone else's. So if you choose to stay with your partner, knowing they have a track record of such behaviors, be realistic; acknowledge relapse is a genuine possibility, no matter how much you hope (and they swear) it won't happen.

Screwing Up

Because human beings screw up so often, I repeatedly ask my clients these three questions:

1. When your partner screws up, how would you ideally respond?

2. When you screw up, how would you ideally like your partner to respond?

3. When either one of you screws up, what would you ideally say or do to handle it effectively, repair, and make amends?

Before answering these questions, get in touch with your values; reflect on the sort of partner you want to be. Think again of "doormats" and "battering rams," "sharks" and "puppy dogs." If you could respond mindfully, in line with your core values, then what would you say and do when one of you screws up? Are you willing to forgive, let go, and move on? Are you willing to make room for your painful feelings, unhook from unhelpful thoughts, and discuss the issue in a way that allows for repairs? And in between those screw-ups, are you willing to apply the principles of positive reinforcement: active appreciation, catch them doing it right, carrot versus stick?

Comedienne Rita Rudner says: "I love being married. It's so great to find that one special person you want to annoy for the rest of your life." She nailed it! So with this in mind, I have a suggestion. Imagine that your partner is a live-in personal trainer—and you have paid them a small fortune to help you develop some important life skills. Their methods are unconventional, and sometimes drive you nuts. But you want to get your money's worth. So what important life skills can your live-in personal trainer help you develop?

An intimate relationship brings problems, difficulties, and issues in all shapes and forms. But with the right attitude, they become an opportunity not only for your own personal growth, but also to strengthen and deepen the bonds with your partner. The attitude required is *willingness*. Willingness to learn, grow, and adapt. Willingness to approach your differences and find constructive, caring ways of either resolving or accepting them. Willingness to be flexible and adaptable amidst the ever-changing circumstances of life.

Willingness to connect with, care for, and contribute to your partner—even when the going gets tough.

Tying It All Together

One reading of this book is nowhere near enough for it all to sink in. Please use it as reference book: return to it often to revisit ideas, repeat exercises, and refresh your memory. (My hope is that you can open it up at random and always find something that's personally relevant and useful.) A few useful things to remember:

- Love and pain are intimate dance partners; they go hand-in-hand.

- You can't always get what you want.

- There's no such thing as the perfect partner.

- Complex issues don't have simple answers.

- You can't *control* your partner; but you *can* control your own behavior and use it to *constructively influence* your partner.

- The carrot is more effective than the stick.

- Conflict is inevitable. But good communication, assertiveness, making repairs, and being compassionate will make it much less destructive.

- Feelings of love come and go; actions of love can be taken in any moment.

We could easily expand this list to several pages, but the essence of the book—to repair, strengthen, and enrich your relationship—can be summarized in three main ideas:

Be present. Engage with your partner; give them your full attention; actively notice and appreciate what they bring to your life.

Open up. Unhook from unhelpful thoughts and difficult feelings; give them plenty of room; allow them to freely flow through you.

Do what matters. Take action, guided by your values; choose those toward moves, over and over again.

Parting Words

Love is a great adventure. It brings wonder and fear, pleasure and pain, suffering and joy. Appreciate this adventure while it lasts. Make the most of it. Learn from it. Grow from it. And when the going gets tough, treat yourself kindly. And keep in mind the words of the great poet, Rainer Maria Rilke: "For one human being to love another: that is perhaps the most difficult of our tasks; the ultimate, the last test and proof, the work for which all other work is but preparation."

If All Else Fails: How to Leave Your Relationship

I hope that by applying the principles in this book you resolve your issues, reconcile your differences, and deepen and strengthen your relationship. Sadly, sometimes it just doesn't work out that way. Now obviously reading this book does not exhaust the many possibilities for help. For example, many couples find a therapist, coach, or counselor can be very helpful, as can individual therapy. Nonetheless, sometimes no matter how hard you try, you just can't seem to make it work. Maybe your partner continues to undermine your rights, or neglect your needs, or rely on destructive tactics; or maybe you both just have very different ideas of the life you want to lead; or maybe your wounds are simply too deep to heal.

So if you've reached that point of no return, and breaking up is the right choice for you, consider how to effectively leave the relationship. Most people leave in a state of DRAIN: disconnected, reactive, avoidant, inside-the-mind, neglecting their values. This usually makes for a very ugly and extremely painful breakup. However, if you leave mindfully, unhooking from unhelpful stories, making room for your feelings, getting present, and acting on your values, the breakup is likely to be much smoother.

An amicable separation or divorce is better for everyone involved, especially if children are involved. So, if you choose to leave, then what do you want to stand for as you do so? Some people stand for revenge, bitterness, hostility; for dragging the kids through the courts; for hurting others, no matter what the cost. Others stand for something they can be proud of when they look back on this difficult period of their life—such as honesty, courage, fairness, kindness, and consideration.

Self-care and self-protection are also important values, so if you're going to leave, make sure to look after yourself. For example, make sure you've got at least one support person (ideally more)—someone you can trust and rely on to help you through this difficult time. And if you're the one moving out, plan the logistics in advance: Where are you going to stay? Do you have a bank account in your own name, with enough funds to tide you over? What will you do for transport? And so on.

Also consider: As you're doing all this, what stories would it help to unhook from? Revenge stories are especially seductive: "They've hurt me, so I'll hurt them!" Your mind says that revenge will make you feel better, but in truth, this is highly unlikely; even if revenge gives you short-term satisfaction, you're likely to regret it later. So why invest your time, energy, and money on a bitter, hostile, drawn-out, tempestuous breakup, when there's no long-term benefit?

Also keep in mind that every painful situation provides you with an opportunity to further develop your ACT skills. So look for the gold amongst the garbage. Ask yourself, how can I learn and grow and develop from this? How might my own experience benefit others that I care about?

Return again and again to the core principles: be present, open up, live by your values. They are useful for every stage of a relationship: the beginning, the middle, and the end. And that goes for every relationship, including the most important one of all: the relationship you have with yourself. So tune into your values of kindness and caring, and practice self-compassion. And not just once, but over and over. There are difficult times ahead, so you'll need plenty of it.

Resources

Free Resources

In addition to "ACT with Love: Extra Bits," there's a huge treasure trove of free materials—including audio recordings, e-books, handouts and worksheets, YouTube videos, book chapters, articles, blogs, and published studies—available on the "Free Resources" page of thehappinesstrap.com.

Online Resources

The Happiness Trap: eight-week online program

This is a personal growth program for well-being and vitality, inspired by Russ's million-copy bestseller, *The Happiness Trap*. It's a beautifully filmed (and very entertaining) online course, suitable for pretty much anyone and everyone who wishes to build a richer, fuller life.

Online training for therapists, counselors, and coaches

I have created a range of online courses for professional training in ACT, from beginner to advanced level. They cover everything from trauma, depression, and anxiety disorders to treating adolescents, grief and loss, and brief interventions. They are available at www.imlearningact.com.

ACT Companion: The Happiness Trap app

Australian psychologist Anthony Berrick created this excellent smartphone app. It's loaded with cool ACT tools, including the choice point, and contains over two hours of audio recordings—some with my voice, some with Anthony's.

Facebook groups

The Happiness Trap Online Facebook group is a supportive and welcoming community of people who have either read the book or done the online program.

The ACT Made Simple Facebook group is for health professionals only—coaches, counsellors, therapists, doctors, nurses and others who use ACT as part of their work.

Other Books by Russ Harris

The Happiness Trap: How to Stop Struggling and Start Living (2nd edition) by Russ Harris

This million-copy bestseller, translated into more than thirty languages, takes you step-by-step through applying ACT in your life, to overcome depression, stress, and anxiety, and build genuine happiness from the inside out.

The Happiness Trap Pocketbook: How to Stop Struggling and Start Living by Russ Harris and Bev Aisbett

A fun, comic-book version of the original—especially for teenagers and adults who are not into reading. (In North America it's alternatively titled *The Illustrated Happiness Trap*.)

The Reality Slap: How to Survive and Thrive When Life Hits Hard (2nd edition) by Russ Harris

An ACT-based self-help book for grief, loss, and crisis, with a major emphasis on self-compassion.

When Life Hits Hard: How to Transcend Grief, Crisis, and Loss with Acceptance and Commitment Therapy

This is the same book as *The Reality Slap* (2nd edition) mentioned before. It was released under a different title in North America.

ACT Made Simple: An Easy-to-Read Primer on Acceptance and Commitment Therapy (2nd edition)

The world's best selling textbook on ACT, with translations into twenty languages. A classic in the field of psychotherapy literature.

Trauma-Focused ACT: A Practitioner's Guide to Working with Mind, Body, and Emotion Using Acceptance and Commitment Therapy

This textbook for therapists covers in depth how to use ACT with all types of trauma-related issues.

References

Bowlby, J. 1969. *Attachment and Loss*. New York: Basic Books.

Ciarrochi, J., A. Bailey, and R. Harris. 2014. *The Weight Escape: How to Stop Dieting and Start Living*. Boston: Shambhala Publications.

Gottman, J., and N. Silver. 1999. *The Seven Principles of Making Marriage Work*. New York: Three Rivers Press.

Hayes, S. C., K. Strosahl, and K. G. Wilson. 1999. *Acceptance and Commitment Therapy: An Experiential Approach to Behavior Change*. New York: Guilford.

Neff, K. D. 2003. "Self-Compassion: An Alternative Conceptualization of a Healthy Attitude Toward Oneself." *Self and Identity*, 2: 85–102.

Nhat Hanh, T. 1976. *The Miracle of Mindfulness!* Boston: Beacon Press.

Weintraub, S. 2001. *Silent Night: The Story of the World War I Christmas Truce*. New York: The Free Press.

Real change *is* possible

For more than forty-five years, New Harbinger has published proven-effective self-help books and pioneering workbooks to help readers of all ages and backgrounds improve mental health and well-being, and achieve lasting personal growth. In addition, our spirituality books offer profound guidance for deepening awareness and cultivating healing, self-discovery, and fulfillment.

Founded by psychologist Matthew McKay and Patrick Fanning, New Harbinger is proud to be an independent, employee-owned company. Our books reflect our core values of integrity, innovation, commitment, sustainability, compassion, and trust. Written by leaders in the field and recommended by therapists worldwide, New Harbinger books are practical, accessible, and provide real tools for real change.

 **newharbinger**publications

Russ Harris is an internationally acclaimed acceptance and commitment therapy (ACT) trainer; and author of the best-selling ACT-based self-help book, *The Happiness Trap*, which has sold more than one million copies and been published in thirty languages. He is widely renowned for his ability to teach ACT in a way that is simple, clear, and fun—yet extremely practical.

MORE BOOKS from
NEW HARBINGER PUBLICATIONS

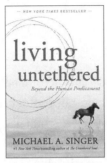

ADULT DAUGHTERS OF NARCISSISTIC MOTHERS

Quiet the Critical Voice in Your Head, Heal Self-Doubt, and Live the Life You Deserve

978-1648480096 / US $18.95

LIVING UNTETHERED

Beyond the Human Predicament

978-1648480935 / US $18.95

ACT DAILY JOURNAL

Get Unstuck and Live Fully with Acceptance and Commitment Therapy

978-1684037377 / US $18.95

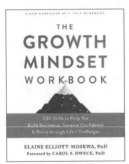

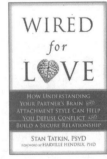

THE EMOTIONALLY EXHAUSTED WOMAN

Why You're Feeling Depleted and How to Get What You Need

978-1648480157 / US $18.95

THE GROWTH MINDSET WORKBOOK

CBT Skills to Help You Build Resilience, Increase Confidence, and Thrive through Life's Challenges

978-1-684038299 / US $24.95

WIRED FOR LOVE

How Understanding Your Partner's Brain and Attachment Style Can Help You Defuse Conflict and Build a Secure Relationship

978-1608820580 / US $18.95

newharbingerpublications

1-800-748-6273 / newharbinger.com

(VISA, MC, AMEX / prices subject to change without notice)

Follow Us 🟦📘▶🐦📷📌in

Don't miss out on new books from New Harbinger.
Subscribe to our email list at **newharbinger.com/subscribe**